CHILD CARE LAW

A SUMMARY

SCOTLAND

Alexandra Plumtree

BAAF
ADOPTION
& FOSTERING

Published by
British Association for Adoption & Fostering
(BAAF)
Saffron House
6–10 Kirby Street
London EC1N 8TS
www.baaf.org.uk

Charity registration 275689 (England and Wales) and SC039337 (Scotland)

© Alexandra Plumtree and BAAF, 2014

British Library Cataloguing in Publication Data
A catalogue record for this book is available from the British Library

ISBN 978 1 907585 76 0

Project management by Jo Francis, Publications, BAAF

Designed and typeset by Helen Joubert Design

Printed in Great Britain by TJ International Ltd, Cornwall

Trade distribution by Turnaround Publisher Services, Unit 3, Olympia Trading Estate, Coburg Road, London N22 6TZ

BAAF is the leading UK-wide membership organisation for all those concerned with adoption, fostering and child care issues.

Contents

Note about the author

Alexandra Plumtree qualified as a Scottish solicitor in 1977. She has worked in private practice and as a children's reporter, and has extensive experience of public and private law for children and families in Scotland. She was the Legal Consultant with BAAF Scotland from 1994 to 2013, and the Independent Legal Adviser to the Scottish Executive's Adoption Policy Review Group from 2001 to 2005. She is a freelance legal consultant and also writes for W. Green and Butterworths/LexisNexis.

Preface

This book is the sixth and further revised edition of BAAF's existing title, *Child Care Law: A summary of the law in Scotland*. It takes account of the changes since the previous edition in 2005, particularly those arising from the Adoption and Children (Scotland) Act 2007, the Protection of Vulnerable Groups (Scotland) Act 2007, the Public Services Reform (Scotland) Act 2010 and the Children's Hearings (Scotland) Act 2011, along with supporting regulations and court rules.

The most recent legislation is the Children and Young People (Scotland) Act 2014, which was passed by the Scottish Parliament on 19 February 2014. It covers a wide range of child care matters, and some of the provisions stand alone, while others amend existing legislation, such as the Children (Scotland) Act 1995. At the time of writing (February 2014), implementation dates and subordinate legislation are not available, but I have tried to outline some of the important provisions to give an idea of the Act's impact.

As with previous editions, this book is not a detailed legal textbook about what is a wide-reaching area of law. Rather, it aims to provide a basic framework of the law for those who do not need to know more *and* a starting point for those who have to look further. Statutory references are given throughout the text with abbreviations listed in Chapter 1. There is a list of further reading and useful websites.

I should like to thank all of those who have given and continue to give me the benefit of their views on the issues of law and practice that are constantly arising in this area of law. I am grateful to Professor Kenneth McK Norrie for his help with the Human Fertilisation Act 2008. Any mistakes are, of course, mine. I am also grateful to all my former colleagues in BAAF Scotland for their help and support, and to Jo Francis and Shaila Shah in BAAF's Publications Department in London.

I have tried to state the law as at 21 February 2014.

Alexandra Plumtree

1

Introduction and abbreviations

This chapter sets out the main legislative background for child care law in Scotland, and other relevant provisions. It includes an outline of devolution, and relevant legislation. It also gives abbreviations for legislation, etc, and other terms used in the text. Acts, regulations and court rules are listed in date order.

Scots law and devolution

1.1

The **Scotland Act 1998 (the 1998 Act)** established the Scottish Parliament, Holyrood, from July 1999. As a result, Acts applying in Scotland may either be passed by the Westminster Parliament or by Holyrood. Those dated before 1999 will be from Westminster, but those after then could be from either Parliament. Acts with "Scotland" (or a clear reference to Scotland) in their title apply to Scotland, but in other Acts, it is necessary to check the "Extent" section near the end, to find out which part or parts of the UK they apply to.

1.2

The effect of the 1998 Act and devolution is that devolved matters (see para 1.3) may be legislated for in Scotland, but this does not mean that differences from the rest of the UK only arise because of the 1998 Act. Scots Law and the Scottish legal system have always been different from those in the rest of the UK. In particular, for the purposes of this book, child care law is different and always has been.

1.3

Holyrood can only legislate about "devolved" matters, not about anything which is "retained" by Westminster. But the 1998 Act says that unless a matter listed in it is reserved to Westminster, it is devolved to Holyrood.

1.4

Most things which affect day-to-day life are devolved, such as education, social work, health services, local authorities, property law, family law, the police and criminal law. Retained matters, which Holyrood cannot usually pass laws about, include the benefits system, immigration law, employment law, defence, foreign affairs and anti-discrimination law. Holyrood cannot change the basic rules about them, but it can legislate to implement policy and practice in these areas. Conversely, Holyrood can "give back" to Westminster the power to make law on devolved matters, if Members of Scottish Parliament (MSPs) vote for this in a Sewel motion. For example, Holyrood allowed the Adoption and Children Act 2002 to include some provisions for Scotland, although most of the Act does not apply in Scotland. Also, the Civil Partnership Act 2004, passed by Westminster, was allowed to include devolved issues as well as retained ones, so that it covers the whole of the UK, albeit that there are substantial Scottish provisions.

Statutory background

1. 5

Many provisions given here are referred to in more detail in later chapters. Others are relevant to the general application of the law, such as the Human Rights Act 1998.

Conventions and Acts of Parliament

1.6
—

European Convention on Human Rights 1950   **ECHR**

See the HRA 1998 below.

UN Convention on the Rights of the Child 1989   **UNCRC**

Unlike the ECHR, this has not been incorporated into UK law and remains persuasive only. However, the Children and Young People (Scotland) Act 2014 places duties on the Scottish Ministers to consider steps which might achieve 'better or further effect' of the UNCRC, promote public awareness of it and provide a three-yearly report to the Scottish Parliament about steps taken and future plans. There are also duties on a range of public authorities, including local authorities and health boards, to publish three-yearly reports about what steps they have taken to achieve 'better or further effect' of the UNCRC. See below (and the Preface) for more information on the 2014 Act.

Hague Convention on Protection of Children and
Co-operation in Respect of Intercountry Adoption, 1993   Hague Convention

This governs arrangements for foreign adoption between those countries which have ratified it, including the UK. See Chapter 14.

Adoption (Scotland) Act 1978   **1978 Act**

This was the adoption legislation in Scotland before 28 September 2009, when it was replaced by the **Adoption and Children (Scotland) Act 2007** – see below.

Foster Children (Scotland) Act 1984   **1984 Act**

This Act governs private fostering, along with the

Foster Children (Private Fostering) (Scotland) Regulations 1985   1985 Regs

There is also Scottish Government Guidance issued in 2013 – see Chapter 6, Private arrangements, and Chapter 10, Fostering and kinship care.

Human Fertilisation and Embryology Act 1990   1990 Act

This established the Human Fertilisation and Embryology Authority and the regulatory structures for assisted reproduction. It was substantially amended by the **Human Fertilisation and Embryology Act 2008** – see below and Chapter 4.

Age of Legal Capacity (Scotland) Act 1991   1991 Act

This Act sets out the ages at which children and young people attain legal capacity in civil matters. See Chapter 2.

Children (Scotland) Act 1995   1995 Act

This remains the principal Act for private and some public law about children in Scotland, although it no longer deals with the Children's Hearing system. It covers:

- private law in Part I of the Act – see Chapters 2 and 4 of this book;

- local authority public law duties and powers in Chapter 1 of Part II of the Act – see Chapters 7, 8, 9 and 10 of this book;

- exclusion orders, ss.76 to 80 – see Chapter 8 of this book;

- definitions for the provisions in Part II of the Act in s.93.

NB The Act originally amended the 1978 Act, but those provisions (and ss.86 to 89 about parental responsibilities orders) were replaced by the **Adoption and Children (Scotland) Act 2007** (see below) from 28 September 2009. The provisions for the Children's Hearing system were replaced by the **Children's Hearings (Scotland) Act 2011** (see below) from 24 June 2013.

Data Protection Act 1998   DPA 1998

This Act applies to the whole of the UK and governs the keeping and release of personal data held on file about individuals. This includes social work and education information held by local authorities. Individuals are entitled to access personal data held on them and this cannot be shared with others without their consent, although there are exceptions to these rules. The system is very complicated and is monitored by the UK Information Commissioner. Under the subject access provisions, individuals are entitled to seek access to their own personal data in social work files, but all Scottish adoption agency records are specifically exempt from the subject access provisions by regulations. Data protection issues should not be confused with FOI matters – see the **Freedom of Information Act 2000** and the **Freedom of Information (Scotland) Act 2002** below.

Human Rights Act 1998   HRA 1998

This Act gives effect throughout the UK to the rights and freedoms guaranteed under the ECHR. The actions of all public authorities, including courts, local authorities and other agencies, must be compatible with the ECHR.

Adoption (Intercountry Aspects) Act 1999   1999 Act

This is a Westminster Act which first regulated arrangements for intercountry adoption. While much of it has been replaced for Scotland by the **Adoption and Children (Scotland) Act 2007**, it is still relevant, particularly for adoptions from Hague Convention countries.

Freedom of Information Act 2000   FOI Act 2000

Freedom of Information (Scotland) Act 2002   FOI(S) Act 2002

These are about rights to access non-personal data and information held by public authorities. The 2000 Act covers all UK-wide public authorities and those in England, Wales and Northern Ireland, under the Information Commissioner. The 2002 Act covers public authorities based in Scotland, under the Scottish Information Commissioner.

Regulation of Care (Scotland) Act 2001   2001 Act

This established a system for regulation, registration and inspection of a wide range of care services. It set up the Scottish Commission for the Regulation of Care – the Care Commission – and the Scottish Social Services Council. The provisions of the Act about the Care Commission were replaced by the **Public Services Reform (Scotland) Act 2010** from 1 April 2011. See Chapter 5.

Protection of Children (Scotland) Act 2003   POCSA 2003

This introduced a duty on Scottish Ministers to maintain a list of people considered unsuitable to work with children. It was repealed and replaced by the **Protection of Vulnerable Groups (Scotland) Act 2007** from February 2011 – see below and Chapter 2, paragraphs 2.15 to 2.20.

Civil Partnership Act 2004   CPA 2004

This came into force throughout the UK on 5 December 2005. It allows same-sex couples to enter into formal civil partnerships with considerable legal consequences in a wide range of matters, including inheritance, property, taxation and immigration. It has different provisions for the different parts of the UK. It does not have provisions for Scotland about parental responsibilities and rights for children, but see Chapter 4, paragraph 4.23. It did not enable same-sex couples to adopt in the UK, but this has been possible in England and Wales from 30 December 2005 under the 2002 Act and in Scotland from 28 September 2009, under the 2007 Act – see Chapter 13.

Family Law (Scotland) Act 2006   FL(S)A 2006

This covers a range of issues, including parental responsibilities and rights for unmarried fathers (see Chapter 4, paragraph 4.16) and rights for separating unmarried couples.

Equality Act 2006   EA 2006

This established the Equality and Human Rights Commission (EHRC). It replaced the Commission for Racial Equality, the Disability Rights Commission and the Equal Opportunities Commission, which were merged into the EHRC in October 2007.

Adoption and Children (Scotland) Act 2007   AC(S)A 2007

This has been the adoption legislation in Scotland from 28 September 2009, when it replaced the 1978 Act. Earlier adoption legislation goes back to 1930. It also deals with permanence orders. See Chapters 12, 13 and 14.

Protection of Vulnerable Groups (Scotland) Act 2007   PVG(S)A 2007

From February 2011, this replaced the POCSA 2003 and extended the protection system to vulnerable adults. It introduced the PVG scheme for vetting and barring There are lists of people considered unsuitable to work with children and/or protected adults; and there are duties on organisations to refer people for possible inclusion and consequences for all people who work with children or protected adults, whether in employment or on a voluntary basis. See Chapter 2, paragraphs 2.15 to 2.20.

Human Fertilisation and Embryology Act 2008   HFEA 2008

This substantially amended the HFEA 1999. The law about parenthood in assisted reproduction is now in the 2008 Act – see Chapter 4. HFEA matters in Scotland are reserved to Westminster.

Equality Act 2010   EA 2010

This replaced previous anti-discrimination legislation, bringing the provisions into one Act. Among the provisions it replaced were the Race Relations Act 1976, as amended by the Race Relations (Amendment) Act 2000, and the Disability Discrimination Acts 1995 and 2005. The 2010 Act includes provisions obliging public authorities (such as local authorities) to promote racial equality, equal opportunities and good race relations, and to eliminate unlawful discrimination in all their work, including service delivery, policy making and employment. These provisions have clear relevance to all children and family services provided by local authorities. Authorities need to be clear about how all their policies and services affect race equality and other areas of possible discrimination.

Public Services Reform (Scotland) Act 2010   **2010 Act**

Among other reforms, this replaced the Care Commission provisions in the 2001 Act from 1 April 2011 – see Chapter 5.

Children's Hearings (Scotland) Act 2011   **2011 Act**

This is the legislation for the Children's Hearing system and came into force on 24 June 2013. It replaced the 1995 Act hearing provisions, and there is a lot of secondary legislation, including provisions about secure accommodation. See Chapter 11.

Children and Young People (Scotland) Act 2014   **2014 Act**

This was introduced into the Scottish Parliament in April 2013 and was passed in February 2014. It amends and adds to a range of provisions about children's services and will affect a number of child care matters dealt with in this book, as it is brought into force. See the comments in the Preface.

Regulations, etc

1.7

Support and Assistance of Young People Leaving Care (Scotland) Regulations 2003, SS1 2003/608   **Leaving Care Regs 2003**

These set out detailed duties on local authorities to those young people for whom they have "aftercare" duties under s.29 of the 1995 Act, as amended by the 2001 Act. There is also Guidance, see below. See Chapter 9, paragraph 9.12.

Adoption Support Services and Allowances (Scotland) Regulations 2009, SSI 2009/152   **Ad Supp Regs 2009**

These cover arrangements for adoption support services and adoption allowances – see Chapter 13.

Adoption Agencies (Scotland) Regulations 2009, SSI 2009/154, as amended by the Adoption Agencies (Scotland) Amendment Regulations 2010, SSI 2010/172, the Public Services Reform (Scotland) Act 2010 (Consequential Modifications) Order 2011, SS1 2011/211, and the Children's Hearings (Scotland) Act 2011 (Modification of Subordinate Legislation) Order 2013, SSI 2013/147

Ad Ag Regs 2009

These set out the rules for the running of adoption services (but not adoption support) by local authority and voluntary adoption agencies, including planning for children who are to be adopted. See Chapter 13.

Adoptions with a Foreign Element (Scotland) Regulations 2009, SSI 2009/182, amended by the Adoptions with a Foreign Element (Scotland) Amendment Regulations 2010, SSI 2010/173 and the Adoptions with a Foreign Element (Scotland) Amendment Regulations 2011, SSI 2011/159

Foreign Adoption Regs 2009

These are about arrangements for children involved in foreign or overseas adoptions. There are two types of foreign adoptions: where children from overseas are adopted into Scotland, usually referred to as intercountry adoptions; and where Scottish children leave the UK for adoption in overseas countries. See Chapter 14.

Looked After Children (Scotland) Regulations 2009, SSI 2009/210, amended by the Looked After Children (Scotland) Amendment Regulations 2009, SSI 2009/290, the Public Services Reform (Scotland) Act 2010 (Consequential Modifications) Order 2011, SS1 2011/211, the Looked After Children (Scotland) Amendment Regulations 2013, SSI 2013/14, and the Children's Hearings (Scotland) Act 2011 (Modification of Subordinate Legislation) Order 2013, SSI 2013/147

LAC Regs 2009

These set out the rules for all looked after children, public fostering, kinship care and arrangements between local authorities and registered fostering services. They include provisions for children's plans and medical assessments, looked after children (LAC) reviews and arrangements for fostering and kinship carers. They have been substantially amended for the

2011 Act by SSI 2013/147 and are likely to be amended in due course for the 2014 Act. See Chapters 9 and 10.

Adoption (Disclosure of Information and Medical Information about Natural Parents) (Scotland) Regulations 2009, SSI 2009/268   Ad Info Regs 2009

These set out the rules for accessing information from adoption agency records, which are exempt from the subject access provisions of the DPA 1998. They also allow for the sharing of medical information about a child who may be adopted, even without parental permission.

Children's Hearings (Scotland) Act 2011 (Rules of Procedure in Children's Hearings) Rules 2013, SSI 2013/194   CH Rules 2013

These govern the organisation and running of hearings – see Chapter 11.

Court rules

1.8

NB These are all available on the Scottish Courts website – see Further Reading.

Act of Sederunt (Sheriff Court Ordinary Cause Rules) 1993 (as amended)   OCR

These are for a wide range of sheriff court cases called Ordinary Causes. They include applications in family cases under the 1995 Act, such as residence and contact orders, and divorce proceedings. These rules govern the preparation of court reports which may be ordered in these cases. See Chapter 4.

Act of Sederunt (Rules of the Court of Session) 1994 (as amended)   RCS

These are court rules for Court of Session cases, with Forms. They cover all cases, including *Family Actions*, Chapter 49, and *Adoption*, Chapter 67.

Act of Sederunt (Child Care and Maintenance Rules) 1997   **AS 1997**

These are the sheriff court rules for a range of child care and other proceedings. Chapter 3 of the rules covers children's hearing cases in the sheriff court (see Chapter 11 in this book) and applications for CAOs, CPOs and EOs (see Chapter 8 in this book). Chapter 2 of the rules covers applications under the HFEA 2008 (see Chapter 4 in this book).

Schedule to the Act of Sederunt (Sheriff Court Rules Amendment) (Adoption and Children (Scotland) Act 2007) 2009, SSI 2009/284, as amended   **Sheriff Court Adoption Rules 2009**

These are the court rules for applications in the sheriff court under the 2007 Act, for adoption, permanence orders and related matters.

Guidance

1.9

There is a range of guidance which is relevant to child care law. They are available on the Scottish Government website – see Further Reading. The principal ones are:

- **Scotland's Children: The Children (Scotland) Act 1995, Regulations and Guidance, Volume 1: Support and Protection for Children and their Families**   **1995 Act Guidance**

- **Supporting Young People Leaving Care in Scotland: Regulations and Guidance on Services for Young People Ceasing to be Looked After by Local Authorities** issued on 31 March 2004   **Leaving Care Guidance**

- **National Guidance for Child Protection in Scotland 2010** issued on 13 December 2010, amended and added to including for the 2011 Act and the Forced Marriage etc (Protection and Jurisdiction) (Scotland) Act 2011. Publication of a refreshed version is anticipated in early 2014 and will be published on the Scottish Government and WithScotland websites – see Further Reading.   **Child Protection Guidance**

- **Guidance on the Looked After Children (Scotland) Regulations 2009 and the Adoption and Children (Scotland) Act 2007** issued on 10 March 2011
2007 Act Guidance

- **Private Fostering in Scotland – Practice Guidance for Local Authority Children's Services** issued on 29 November 2013
Private Fostering Guidance

Standards

1.10

Under the 2001 Act, many **National Care Standards** were produced, and these are still applied under the 2010 Act. They include:

National Care Standards: Foster Care and Family Placement Services — **Fostering Standards**

National Care Standards: Adoption Agencies — **Adoption Standards**

See Chapters 5, 6, 10, 12 and 13.

OTHER ABBREVIATIONS

Legislation

1.11

- 1937 Act — Children and Young Persons (Scotland) Act 1937
- 1968 Act — Social Work (Scotland) Act 1968
- 1975 Act — Children Act 1975
- 1985 Act — Family Law (Scotland) Act 1985
- 1986 Act — Law Reform (Parent and Child) (Scotland) Act 1986
- FLA 1986 — Family Law Act 1986

- 1989 Act   Children Act 1989
- CSA 1991   Child Support Act 1991
- CP(S)A 1995   Criminal Procedure (Scotland) Act 1995
- ASBA 2004   Antisocial Behaviour etc (Scotland) Act 2004
- FM Act 2011   Forced Marriage etc (Protection and Jurisdiction) (Scotland) Act 2011

Other terms

- APRG   Adoption Policy Review Group
- ASBO   Antisocial Behaviour Order – see Chapter 11
- CAO   Child Assessment Order – see Chapter 8
- CPO   Child Protection Order – see Chapter 8
- CSO   Compulsory Supervision Order – see Chapter 11
- EO   Exclusion Order – see Chapter 8
- PO or POA   Permanence Order or Permanence Order with authority for adoption – see Chapter 12
- PRRs   parental responsibilities and/or parental rights
- PVG Scheme   Protection of Vulnerable Groups Scheme – see Chapter 2
- r. or rr.   specific rule(s)
- reg. or regs.   specific regulation(s)
- RFS   registered fostering service – see Chapter 10
- s. or ss.   specific section(s) of an Act

2

Principles and themes

This chapter deals with general themes and principles in the law of Scotland relating to children, some of which are in the 1995, 2007 and 2011 Acts.

Definition of "child"

2.1
—

There is no single definition of "child" in the law of Scotland. Whether a young person is a child or not will depend on the particular legislation and/or circumstances. However, as a rule of thumb, 16-year-olds in Scotland may do most things legally except buy alcohol (18) or drive (17). In private disputes about children between parents and other carers, the law usually regulates the position only up to 16, although parents are obliged to pay maintenance for their children beyond that time and until they finish all education. Where a child is looked after by the local authority, that care can last up to 18 and there is provision for after-care beyond that.

Some other definitions

2.2
—

There is a distinction between criminal and civil law. Criminal law is self-explanatory and, for the purposes of this book, anything which is not criminal is treated as civil. The Children's Hearing system straddles civil and criminal law and has been described as a *sui generis* system, that is, of its own kind, unique.

WW v Kennedy 1988 SCLR 236 at 239

2.3
___

Another distinction is made between private and public law. For the purposes of this book, private law relates to matters between private individuals and their rights and responsibilities in relation to each other. Public law deals with the ways in which society and the state become involved in the lives of children and families. Adoption law straddles this divide, as it is a private law action in the courts, but often (not always) comes about because of public law intervention by a local authority.

Principles to be applied

2.4
___

The 1995 Act introduced or re-stated principles which apply to most decisions in the areas of law it covered. Those areas included private law, local authority duties, child protection measures, the Children's Hearing system and adoption. The 2007 and 2011 Acts have replaced some of the provisions covered by the 1995 Act, but the principles (or "considerations") have been carried forward into these subsequent Acts. The principles are set out below.

Child's welfare to be paramount consideration or concern

2.5
___

This was not a completely new test in all types of cases in the 1995 Act, but is the test which now applies in court decisions, children's hearing decisions and local authority and adoption agency decisions about welfare in the areas listed in paragraph 2.4 above. In private law cases this has been the test since 1986, but in adoption matters the test prior to the 1995 Act was "first consideration" of the child's welfare, and there was no specific test in other matters. Under the 2007 Act, the test in adoption is that the child's welfare throughout the child's life shall be of paramount consideration. In POA cases, the courts have also applied this principle. In all other cases, including applications for POs, the test is the child's welfare throughout childhood. In addition to this duty, the 2014 Act contains a new 'wellbeing' duty on local authorities in providing services to children in need, looked after children and children receiving continuing care – see Chapter 7, paragraph 7.19.

1995 Act, s.11(7)(a) and (7A) to (7E) and s.17(1)(a); 2007 Act, s.14(3) and s.84(4); 2011 Act, s.25; Looked After Regs 2009; case law in relation to POAs; and 2014 Act, ss.95 and 96

Consideration of the child's views

2.6

Courts, children's hearings, local authorities and adoption agencies all have a duty to allow children to express their views about their situations, and to take account of these views in their decisions. While this had been good practice in many areas, the 1995 Act formally introduced it as a duty in these situations, and the 2007 and 2011 Acts continue the duty. *There is no lower age limit*. The 1995, 2007 and 2011 Acts all say that children who are 12 or over are presumed to have views, and this clearly implies that younger children can have views although they are not presumed to have them. It is necessary *in all cases* to find out:

- if children have views;
- whether they wish to express them; and if so,
- to take account of the views.

However, this does not mean the same thing as doing exactly what children want.

1995 Act, s.6(1), s.11(7)(b) and (10), s.17(3) and (4) and s.25(5); 2007 Act, s.14(4)(b) and (8) and s.84(5)(a), (b)(i) and (6); 2011 Act, s.27; Looked After Children Regs 2009

Minimum necessary intervention

2.7

This principle is sometimes called the "no order" principle. It states that no

court order or children's hearing order shall be made unless the court/hearing thinks that making an order is better for the child than not making it. This does not mean that making an order is a "last resort". It means that the court or hearing must be certain that an order is necessary for the child's welfare, and that the order it is making is the best one. If the child's welfare can be secured as paramount consideration without an order or with less of an order, that is what should be done. Adoption agencies have a similar duty when they are making any decisions relating to the adoption of a child: they must consider alternatives.

1995 Act, s.11(7)(a); 2007 Act, s.14(6) and (7), s.28(2) and s.84(3); 2011 Act, ss.28 and 29

Consideration of religious persuasion, racial, cultural and linguistic heritage

2.8

This principle was introduced by the 1995 Act and is also in the 2007 Act, but does not cover all areas of law. It applies to decisions which the local authority make in relation to children whom they are "looking after" or whom they are treating as 'in need'. It is also a duty on adoption agencies and courts in any decisions relating to adoption. There is no mention of it in Part I of the 1995 Act, about private law. However, there is case law indicating that these matters are important and need to be considered in private law cases. The principle did not apply to the hearing system in the 1995 Act and is not in the 2011 Act either.

1995 Act, s.17(4)(c) and s.22(2); 2007 Act, s.14(4)(c) and s.84(5)(b)(ii); *Osborne v Matthan* 1997 SLT 811 (18 October 1996).

Capacity of children: criminal and civil

2.9

The age of criminal capacity in Scotland is eight. Since 28 March 2011, a child under 12 cannot be prosecuted in the adult criminal courts, following implementation of s.52 of the Criminal Justice and Licensing (Scotland) Act 2010. However, a child aged between 8 and 12 may still be referred to a children's hearing on offence grounds – see Chapter 11.

CP(S)A 1995, s.41A, inserted by the 2010 Act, s.52

2.10

The age of civil capacity in Scotland is generally 16, but with specific exceptions. These are that a child under 16:

- may carry out normal transactions (e.g. buy sweets, trainers, etc);

- may make a will if 12 or over;

- must be asked if he or she consents to adoption if 12 or over (unless incapable);

- must be the person to consent or otherwise to medical, dental and surgical treatment if, in the opinion of the qualified medical practitioner, he or she is capable of understanding the nature and possible consequences of the treatment;

- may instruct a solicitor in any civil matter if he or she has a general understanding of what it means to do so.

The most striking of these are the rights to consent to medical treatment and to instruct a solicitor.

1991 Act, s.1 and s 2, particularly s.2(4), (4A) and (4B)

Medical consent for children

2.11

Consent to medical treatment must come from the young person under 16 *when* a medical practitioner considers her or him to be capable of understanding the nature and consequences of the treatment – see paragraph 2.10. It is considered that the right to consent includes the right to refuse to consent. Parental consent is not needed in these circumstances and cannot override the child's consent or refusal, but it is good practice to work with the family as a whole if possible. Nothing in the 2011 Act interferes with the child's capacity under the 1991 Act. The law is different from that in England and Wales.

1991 Act, s.2(4); 2011 Act, s.186

Mental health

2.12
___

Mental health law in Scotland has been contained in the Mental Health (Care and Treatment) (Scotland) Act 2003 since 5 October 2005. There is no lower age limit and it may be used for children and young people. The 2003 Act has more provisions than the previous legislation to take account of the welfare and interests of children and other patients.

Mental Health (Care and Treatment) (Scotland) Act 2003

Working co-operatively

2.13
___

Good co-operative working between all individuals and agencies making decisions about children or working with them and their families is positively encouraged by the 1995 Act, in private and public law cases, and this has continued under subsequent legislation, including the 2014 Act. There is an expectation that parents will work together and with their children in all decisions about welfare, even if the parents themselves do not get on. There is an expectation that, where the local authority is involved with children and families, they will work co-operatively and in partnership with them.

Local authority

2.14

'Local authority' is defined in the 1995 and 2007 Acts as meaning the whole local authority and all its departments, not just the social work department. This was a change from the position under the 1968 Act. It means that the whole local authority are obliged to carry out responsibilities, duties, etc, when they are owed to children and families, whether the children are 'in need', 'looked after' or requiring other services. The 2011 Act does not have a specific definition of the words 'local authority', but it should be taken to mean the same as in the 1995 Act. In addition, all children who are subject to CSOs are 'looked after' in terms of the 1995 Act, so its definition applies.

1995 Act, s.93(1); 2007 Act, s.119(1); 1995 Act, s.17(6) as amended by the 2011 Act, Schedule 5, para 2(4)

The Disclosure system for criminal record checks, the PVG Scheme and vetting and barring

2.15

The Police Act 1997 introduced a new system for disclosing criminal history information to individuals and organisations for employment and other purposes. Disclosure Scotland is the body which arranges for checks. The POCSA 2003 came into force in 2005, and required many people to have a criminal record check when "working" with children, in both paid employment or on a voluntary basis. It also introduced a list, to be kept by Scottish Ministers, of people who were unsuitable to work with children; and duties on courts, employers, voluntary organisations and others to refer people for possible listing.

Police Act 1997, Part V; POCSA 2003

6

2.16

On 28 February 2011, the PVG(S)A 2007 repealed and replaced the POCSA 2003 and extended the system of criminal record checks and listing to those working with protected adults. There are now two separate lists, for people considered unsuitable to work with children and/or with protected adults. The PVG(S)A 2007 introduced the PVG Scheme for vetting people working with children and protected adults and barring those on one or other of the lists. There are also duties on organisations to refer people for possible inclusion on one or other of the lists.

PVG(S)A 2007

2.17

All disclosure checks in Scotland are carried out by Disclosure Scotland under the PVG(S)A 2007 and under Part V of the Police Act 1997. Disclosure Scotland provides:

- PVG Scheme disclosures under the PVG(S)A 2007, for Scheme members;

- Enhanced, Standard and Basic Disclosures under the 1997 Act.

PVG(S)A 2007; Police Act 1997

2.18

The PVG Scheme was established under the PVG(S)A 2007 for those carrying out 'regulated work' (paid or unpaid) with children (under 18) and also with protected adults. Membership of the PVG Scheme gives a disclosure, a PVG Scheme Record, with the same comprehensive information as an Enhanced Disclosure (see below). It also allows Record Updates and Membership Statements to be issued after joining, without the need to apply for a new full disclosure every time; and for automatic updating of the Scheme member's record if any new vetting information arises.

PVG(S)A 2007

2.19

Not everyone is entitled to join the PVG Scheme. When that is the case, a 1997 Act disclosure may/will be available – see paragraph 2.20 below. There is extensive information on Disclosure Scotland's website (see Further Reading) about which checks are available and for whom. In particular, there is the *Updated Guidance on Foster Care, Kinship Care and Adoption*, published in May 2012, which provides a guide as to who may be checked and how in this area of work. Further Reading has information about how to access this.

PVG(S)A 2007; Police Act 1997

2.20

1997 Act Disclosures provide different levels of check, depending on the type.

- An **Enhanced Disclosure** contains all conviction information, whether spent or unspent under the Rehabilitation of Offenders Act 1974, and any other non-conviction information considered relevant by the police or other Government bodies.

- A **Standard Disclosure** contains all conviction information, spent and unspent, including cautions, but no non-conviction information or police intelligence.

- A **Basic Disclosure** contains only convictions unspent under the 1974 Act.

Anyone can apply for a Basic Disclosure for himself/herself but the others may only be applied for by organisations and those entitled to seek them for people doing certain work or holding certain posts.

Police Act 1997; Rehabilitation of Offenders Act 1974

3

Scottish courts and the criminal system

This chapter outlines briefly the Scottish court structure and explains some points about the Scottish criminal system in general. Different decisions are made in different courts. Who makes a decision and the procedure used depends on which court is dealing with a case.

The court system

3.1

The Scottish court system is reasonably straightforward. There are three courts which deal with civil matters:

- Sheriff Courts

- Court of Session

- Supreme Court (formerly the Appellate Committee of the House of Lords)

And there are three courts which deal with criminal matters:

- Justice of the Peace Courts, including the Stipendiary Magistrate Court in Glasgow

- Sheriff Courts

- High Court

In addition, however, some criminal matters may be appealed from the High Court to the Supreme Court, in certain circumstances.

3.2

All courts are public authorities under the HRA 1998, so all court decisions must take account of the ECHR.

HRA 1998

3.3

The sheriff court operates in civil, children's hearing and criminal cases and deals with the widest variety of matters. Scotland is divided into six Sheriffdoms and each Sheriffdom has a Sheriff Principal. There are 49 sheriff courts, each of which has a court where a sheriff sits regularly. Sheriffs are either permanent judges, or part-time ones. Both of these have to be legally qualified and have had a number of years' experience. Honorary sheriffs are appointed locally to deal with certain matters when there is a shortage of other sheriffs. They are usually not legally qualified and have very limited powers.

3.4

Sheriffs Principal and sheriffs are addressed as "My Lord" or "My Lady" in court and "Sheriff Principal" or "Sheriff" when off the bench.

Civil courts

The sheriff court

3.5

The sheriff court deals with a wide variety of civil matters. Only the sheriff court can deal with children's hearing proof cases and initial appeals from children's hearings. The sheriff court deals with many cases of divorce, disputes about children, permanence orders and adoption, although these can also be raised in the Court of Session.

3.6

An appeal from a sheriff can go either to the Sheriff Principal for that area or straight to the Court of Session. If there is an appeal to the Sheriff Principal, there may be a further appeal on to the Court of Session. Where a case is started, and where an appeal goes, are decisions for the person raising the case and the person who appeals.

The Court of Session

3.7

This court deals with civil cases from the beginning, and also appeals in civil cases. It sits only in Edinburgh. The judges are legally qualified and are the same as those who sit in the High Court of Justiciary. They may be permanent or temporary appointments and are addressed as "My Lord" or "My Lady".

3.8

If a case is started in the Court of Session, it is heard by a single judge in the "Outer House". If the court is sitting as an appeal court, a group of three or more judges sits to hear the case in the "Inner House". This deals with appeals from sheriffs, Sheriffs Principal and the Outer House.

3.9

The senior judge in Scotland and the head of the Scottish legal system is the Lord President of the Court of Session. He is also the Lord Justice General in criminal cases.

The Supreme Court

3.10

There is an appeal in some but not all civil matters from the Inner House of the Court of Session to the Supreme Court. Adoption, PO and POA appeals and appeals in private law disputes about children may go to the Supreme Court, but appeals under the 2011 Act, in children's hearing cases, cannot do so.

3.11

The judges are called Supreme Court Justices (SCJs). Usually five of them hear a case and if it is a Scottish appeal, two of those judges will, by convention, be Scottish. At any one time, there are always two Scottish Justices.

3.12

Prior to the creation of the Supreme Court in 2008, appeals were heard by the Appellate or Judicial Committee of the House of Lords. The judges sat in the House of Lords as Life Peers, but the Supreme Court has separated out the appeal functions from those of Parliament. Justices are no longer automatically made Life Peers, although some individuals may coincidentally be Peers. The Lord Chancellor, who used to be the senior Law Lord in the House of Lords and the speaker there, is a political appointment. He is the head of the legal system for England and Wales, but not of the Scottish legal system.

The Scottish criminal system

3.13

Prosecution in Scotland is carried out by an independent prosecution service. This is headed by the Crown Office and represented locally by procurators fiscal (PFs). The organisation is called the Crown Office and Procurator Fiscal Service (COPFS).

3.14

Decisions to prosecute are made on the basis of the following questions:

- is there sufficient evidence? *and*

- is it in the public interest to prosecute?

The prosecution decides what offence a person will be charged with and which court will deal with the matter. A case is either *summary*, when it is dealt with by a judge alone; or *solemn*, when it is dealt with by a judge and jury. There is no right to jury trial in Scotland.

3.15

In Scotland, the adult criminal system is not used for most cases involving crimes alleged to have been committed by children under 16. The age of criminal capacity is eight but children under 12 can no longer be prosecuted in the courts (see Chapter 2, paragraph 2.9). Even over the age of 12, most children are not prosecuted in the courts. Instead they are referred by the police to the children's reporter, who decides whether to take the case to a children's hearing (see Chapter 11). The major exception to this rule is where a child is charged with a more serious offence, such as a severe assault or murder. In those circumstances the child will be dealt with by the adult criminal system.

CP(S)A 1995, s.41A, inserted by the Criminal Justice and Licensing (Scotland) Act 2010, s.52; 2011 Act

3.16

By and large, the police report children under 16 only to the reporter. They may also report cases to the Procurator Fiscal. If a case is jointly reported, the PF makes the ultimate decision about whether the child is dealt with in the adult system even if he or she is still subject to a CSO in the hearing system.

3.17

The ASBA 2004 introduced various provisions affecting young people under 16. These involve the courts in a civil and criminal capacity, and the hearing system. These are covered below, in Chapter 11, paragraphs 2.42 to 2.47.

ASBA 2004

Criminal courts

The Justice of the Peace Court

3.18

These courts deal only with minor criminal matters. Cases are heard by one or more lay, unqualified justices, sitting with a legally qualified clerk. In Glasgow, the JP Court may be presided over by a stipendiary magistrate, who is legally qualified and sits on his or her own. As in all criminal courts, cases come to Justice of the Peace Courts on the basis of decisions by the prosecution service.

The Sheriff Court

3.19

Sheriff courts deal with the bulk of criminal cases in Scotland. They deal both with summary matters (lesser crimes) where a sheriff sits and hears the case on his or her own; and more serious cases (solemn matters), which are heard by a sheriff sitting with a jury. Again, decisions to take cases to the sheriff court, and whether with or without a jury, are made by the prosecution service.

The High Court of Justiciary

3.20

This is the court which deals with serious criminal trials; and with *all* criminal appeals in Scotland. The judges are the same as those in the Court of Session.

3.21

If the High Court is dealing with a criminal trial, this is done by a single judge sitting with a jury. The court can try all crimes, but usually only deals with very serious ones. Only the High Court can deal with murder, treason and rape. The court goes on circuit round the country, although the number of places it visits is being reduced.

3.22

When the court is hearing appeals, it sits only in Edinburgh. A group of three or more judges will hear criminal appeals against conviction, from the Justice of the Peace Courts and the sheriff courts, as well as from High Court trials. When appeals relate to sentences in lower courts, only two judges usually hear them.

3.23

The High Court of Justiciary is the final court of appeal in Scotland for many criminal matters relating to the facts of convictions, or sentencing. However, appeals to the Supreme Court are possible in relation to alleged breaches of the correct procedures in criminal cases and issues of incompatibility with the ECHR.

Parentage and parental responsibilities and rights – private law

This chapter deals with parentage of children and parental responsibilities and rights in relation to them. It covers who are parents, who has responsibilities and rights, who can get them and how, together with how the court deals with disputes in this area. Parental responsibilities and rights are referred to as PRRs.

Parentage: legal mother and father

4.1

The rules of parentage are about who is considered to be the legal mother or father of a child. These rules do *not* say who has responsibilities and rights for a child – that is covered below, in paragraphs 4.9 onwards.

4.2

The common, non-statutory law did not deal with who was/is the legal mother of a child, because it is only recently that there was any possibility that the gestational mother could be a different person from the genetic mother. In most cases, there is no physical difference. However, the HFEA 2008 says that the carrying, gestational mother is the legal mother, not the genetic mother if she is a different person. So when a child is born as a result of assisted conception, the gestational mother is the legal mother even if she is not the genetic mother. And when a child is born to a surrogate mother, she is the legal mother. The legal genetic mother automatically has PRRs – see below, paragraph 4.14.

HFEA 2008, s.33

4.3

In unassisted conception, the genetic father is the legal father. There may be uncertainty about who is the genetic father (without DNA testing). Unlike the position of mothers, many genetic legal fathers do not have PRRs automatically – see below, paragraphs 4.15 onwards.

4.4

In unassisted conception, the 1986 Act has two presumptions about who is the legal father. A presumption is a general legal rule and may be challenged and rebutted by going to court and proving it untrue in a particular case. In cases about paternity, that is often shown by DNA evidence. The presumptions are:

- a man married to the mother at any time between the conception and the birth of a child is presumed to be the legal, genetic father. He automatically has PRRs and keeps them unless and until the presumption is rebutted in court proceedings and/or they are removed by a court order.

- a man not married to the mother of a child is presumed to be the legal, genetic father *if* both he and the mother acknowledge him as the father *and* the child has been registered as his child. He may or may not have PRRs, depending on when the child's birth was registered – see paragraphs 4.15 and 4.16.

1986 Act, s.5; 1995 Act, s.3 as amended by the 2006 Act, s.23

4.5

If there is a dispute about who is the legal father, a court can be asked to grant an order about paternity or non-paternity, called a Declarator. If a father obtains a Declarator of Paternity, this raises the presumption that he is the legal, genetic father as if his name was on the birth certificate. But it does not give him PRRs. However, if a man married to the legal mother obtains a Declarator of Non-paternity, he loses the PRRs which he had.

1986 Act, s.7

Parentage: assisted conception

4.6

In assisted conception, the gestational mother is the legal mother. However, the rules about who is the legal father or other parent are extremely complex and this is just a basic outline. Under the 2008 Act, a child may have a legal father or another legal parent; that is, the second parent may be a woman who is a partner of the mother.

- If a woman conceives using her partner's sperm, he is the legal father and will have PRRs automatically if they are married or he is registered as the father. If they are not married and he is not registered on the birth certificate as the father, he will be the legal father but have no PRRs.

- If a married woman conceives artificially using sperm which is not her husband's, he is the legal father and will have PRRs, unless it is shown that he did not consent.

- If a woman who is in a civil partnership conceives artificially, her partner is the other legal parent and will have PRRs, unless it is shown that she did not consent.

- If a woman who is married or in a civil partnership conceives artificially, using sperm which is not her husband's, and her husband or civil partner did not consent to this, the child has no legal father or other parent, so long as the donor consented to the use of the sperm in this way.

- If a woman who has a male partner but is not married conceives artificially through a registered clinic, the man may be treated as the legal father if he has no genetic link to the child, provided the 'agreed fatherhood conditions' in s.37 of the HFEA are satisfied. These are largely concerned with the consent of the mother and her partner to treatment and to him being the father. He will not have PRRs automatically unless he is registered on the birth certificate as the father.

- If a woman who has a female partner but is not in a civil partnership conceives artificially through a registered clinic, the partner may be treated as the other legal parent if she has no genetic link to the child, provided the 'agreed female parenthood conditions' in s.44 of the HFEA are satisfied. These are largely concerned with the consent of the mother and her partner to treatment and to the partner being the other parent. She will not have PRRs automatically unless she is registered on the birth certificate as the other legal parent.

- If a woman conceives using sperm or an embryo from a deceased donor, the child has no legal father or other parent, although the deceased may be registered as the father for registration purposes only.

If a legal father does not have PRRs, there are ways in which these can be obtained – see below, paragraphs 4.21 to 4.30. If the other female parent under the 2008 Act does not have PRRs, these may be obtained by an agreement under s.4A or by an order under s.11 of the 1995 Act – see paragraphs 4.21 to 4.30. Section 4A only applies in relation to assisted conception.

HFEA 2008, Part 2, particularly ss.33 to 35, s.42, ss.36 and 37, ss.43 and 44, s.40 and s.46; 1995 Act, s.3 as amended by the 2008 Act, Schedule 6, paragraph 50, s.4 and s.4A inserted by the 2008 Act, Schedule 6, paragraph 51 and s.11

Surrogacy

4.7

When a child is born to a surrogate mother, she is the legal parent and has PRRs. If she is married or a civil partner and her husband or partner agreed to the artificial insemination, he or she is the legal father or other legal parent and also has PRRs. If he or she did not agree, he or she is not the legal father (unless presumed so, though that may be easily overturned) or other legal parent and has no PRRs. If the surrogate mother is not married or a civil partner and the intended father is also the genetic father, he is the legal father and will have PRRs if registered on the birth certificate.

HFEA 2008, ss.33 to 35 and s.42

4.8

The people who commission the surrogacy are often not legal parents and will usually have no PRRs. They may acquire these with the consent of the legal parent(s) by a parental order under the HFEA 2008 if at least one of them is genetically related to the child. If there is no consent or no genetic relationship, they may seek adoption which may be granted even if money has been paid for the surrogacy.

HFEA 2008, s.54; 2007 Act s.29

Parental responsibilities and rights

4.9

The 1995 Act introduced the terminology of parental responsibilities and rights (PRRs), instead of just parental rights. Traditionally, Scots Law treated children as the possession of their parents but the 1995 Act moved away from this, towards treating children as people who have their own rights as well.

4.10

Sections 1 and 2 of the 1995 Act deal with responsibilities and rights, and make it clear that no one should have rights unless they have responsibilities first. The responsibilities are:

- to safeguard and protect the child's welfare;
- to provide guidance;
- to maintain contact if not living with the child; and

- to act as the child's legal representative if need be.

The rights are:

- to have the child living with him or her;

- to control, direct or guide the child;

- to maintain contact if not living with the child; and

- to act as the child's legal representative if need be.

1995 Act, s.1 and s.2

4.11

These rights can be exercised individually by any person having them, without having to obtain the consent of anyone else who also has them. The only exception is that the child cannot be removed from the UK without the consent of every person who has the responsibilities and rights of residence and/or contact *and* is exercising them.

1995 Act, s.2(2), (3) and (6)

Duty to maintain

4.12

The mother and father, whether married or not, are both obliged to maintain a child even if they do not have any responsibilities and rights, unless the child has been adopted or made the subject of an order under the HFEA 2008. This is dealt with by the 1985 Act, not the 1995 Act.

1985 Act, s.1; 2007 Act, s.40; HFEA 2008, s.54

4.13

When parents separate or are otherwise disputing maintenance, courts are now not usually involved. The Child Support Act 1991 established the Child Support Agency and the Child Support Scheme 1993. There is considerable subsequent legislation, which has led to the Child Support Scheme 2003 and, from December 2012, the 2012 Child Maintenance Scheme. This is a complex area of practice and advice in individual cases should be sought from specialists.

Child Support Acts 1991 and 1995, Child Support, Pensions and Social Security Act 2000 and Child Maintenance and Other Payments Act 2008

Who has responsibilities and rights (PRRs) automatically?

4.14

The legal genetic mother of a child always has responsibilities and rights unless and until these are taken away from her by some form of court process such as adoption or a parental order under the HFEA 2008.

1995 Act, s.3

4.15

The legal father only has responsibilities and rights automatically in Scotland if *either*

- he has been or is married to the mother at the time of the child's conception or anytime subsequently; *or*

- his name is on the child's birth certificate *and* the date of registration is on or after 4 May 2006.

1995 Act, s.3, as amended by the 2006 Act, s.23

4.16

Where a couple is married and have children, both parents will have PRRs automatically. If the couple is not married, the genetic father does not have PRRs automatically, unless he is named on the birth certificate and the date of registration is on or after 4 May 2006. If the father is named on the birth certificate prior to that date and/or has a Declarator of Paternity, he does not have PRRs. If he marries the mother at any time after the child's birth, he acquires PRRs if he did not already have them. However, if a man marries a woman with children, but he is not the genetic, legal father, he does not acquire PRRs because of the marriage.

1995 Act, s.3, as amended by the 2006 Act, s.23

4.17

In England and Wales and Northern Ireland, the law was changed in 2003, so unmarried fathers on birth certificates for children born since then have had automatic parental responsibility. These provisions are not retrospective. They need to be remembered when working with families who have moved to Scotland from other parts of the UK.

1989 Act, s.4, as amended by the 2002 Act; Children (Northern Ireland) Order 1995, Article 7 as amended

How can fathers acquire responsibilities and rights (PRRs)?

4.18

A genetic father who does not have PRRs can acquire them by using the agreement provided for in s.4 of the 1995 Act. There is a straightforward form. When it is signed by both genetic parents and sent for registration in the Books of Council and Session (a public register), it gives the father full responsibilities and rights as if he had married the mother. There is a small cost for this, but no formal procedure is involved, and there is no need to go to court. Forms are available from organisations such as Citizens Advice Bureaux. However, they cannot be used by anyone who is not a genetic parent.

1995 Act, s.4

4.19

Section 4 forms provide a straightforward way for couples to give the father PRRs without going to court or being involved in a dispute. There is no need for the couple to live together. Once this agreement is signed and registered, the couple cannot change their minds. The only way to alter the arrangements after that is to go to court.

1995 Act, s.4(4)

4.20

A father with no PRRs can also apply to court under s.11 of the 1995 Act (see paragraphs 4.21 onwards) to obtain them. He has to do this if the mother disagrees with his request for PRRs, and refuses to sign a Section 4 form. He may also want to use s.11 if he does not want all PRRs but only, say, contact.

1995 Act, s.11

Acquiring responsibilities and rights: Section 11 applications and orders

4.21

Section 11 of the 1995 Act allows courts (the sheriff court or Court of Session) to make any type of order about responsibilities and rights, guardianship or a child's property. The court can make an order because it has been asked to do so, or simply because, in any other case, it thinks an order is necessary.

1995 Act, s.11(1), (2) and (3)

4.22

The most common types of s.11 orders are:

- residence orders;
- contact orders;
- specific issue orders;
- interdicts;
- orders giving PRRs;

- orders taking away some or all of a person's PRRs;

- orders appointing or removing someone as a child's guardian.

1995 Act, s.11(2)

4.23

Any person can use this section, provided he or she can claim an interest in the child (but see the restrictions on which orders the court may grant when a child is the subject of a PO or POA – paragraph 4.25). This includes all parents with PRRs, birth fathers without all or some of them and anyone else claiming an interest, including step-parents of children, whether married, civil partners, unmarried or same-sex partners. The only individuals who cannot apply under s.11 in this way are people who have already lost all their PRRs because of an adoption order or an order under the HFEA Acts 1990 or 2008. However, where someone has lost PRRS because of an adoption order, he or she may apply for leave to apply for a contact order under s.11.

1995 Act, s.11 A inserted by the 2007 Act, s.103 and s.11(3)(aa) and (ab) and (4) as inserted and amended by the 2007 Act, s.107, Schedule 2, para 9 (2) and Schedule 3

4.24

Local authorities cannot use this section, but children can use it, as well as adults.

1995 Act, s.11(5)

4.25

When a child is the subject of a PO or POA, a court may not make an order under s.11, unless the application is for an interdict, appointment of a judicial factor for the child or appointment or removal of someone as the child's guardian. This is because the PO or POA will have set out who has what PRRs, and any changes should be applied for in a variation or revocation of the order – see Chapter 12.

1995 Act, s.11A inserted by the 2007 Act, s.103

4.26

The principles outlined in Chapter 2 apply to all s.11 decisions made by courts. This includes taking account of the child's religious persuasion, racial, cultural and linguistic heritage – see Chapter 2, paragraph 2.8.

1995 Act, s.11(7) and (10)

4.27

The law relating to children before the 1995 Act talked about "custody". The term in the 1995 Act is 'residence' although it does *not* mean the same thing. A residence order may be granted to a parent who has PRRs already, *or* it may be granted to someone who does not have any responsibilities and rights to begin with, such as a grandparent or unmarried father.

1995 Act, s.11(12)

4.28

If a residence order is granted to a parent with PRRs, in a divorce or dissolution of civil partnership or other application, the order simply says where the child is to live. It does not take away some or all of the non-residential parent's PRRs, apart from residence, unless the court also orders this for particular reasons. The idea is to encourage parents to work together for their children. This means that the two parents with responsibilities are expected to continue to carry these out, even if they are separated or divorced, or their civil partnership has been dissolved. They both still have rights too.

1995 Act, s.11(11)

4.29

If a residence order is granted to a person who does not already have PRRs, the order allows that person to have all the responsibilities and rights that are needed to care properly for the child. It does not, however, take PRRs (except residence) away from anyone else who already has them, unless and only to the extent the court specifically orders.

1995 Act, s.11(11) and (12)

4.30

Because the principle of minimum necessary intervention applies in these decisions, courts should not grant orders to disputing parents just because parents want them. Courts have to be satisfied, taking the child's welfare as paramount, that the orders wanted are necessary for the child and that it is better to make the orders than not to do so. This represents a move away from giving custodial rights to one parent in a dispute and leaving the other parent with a feeling of very little involvement.

1995 Act, s.11(7)(a)

Interdicts and enforcement

4.31

As has already been mentioned, s.11 orders can include interdicts about children, including an interdict to prevent a child being removed from someone's care, if this is necessary to protect the child.

1995 Act, s.11(2)(f)

4.32

Orders made in Scotland in relation to children are recognised and may be enforced in other parts of the UK. Orders made elsewhere in the UK are also recognised and can be enforced in Scotland.

1986 Act

PRRs for children 'looked after' by the local authority

4.33

The responsibilities of the local authorities themselves for looked after children are dealt with in Chapter 9. However, there is the issue of what parents' PRRs are when children are looked after by a local authority, either on a voluntary basis or because of CSOs from the Children's Hearing system or because there are POs or POAs. The position depends on the basis on which children are looked after.

4.34

Unlike the position in England and Wales in care orders under the 1989 Act, local authorities do *not* acquire any PRRs for looked after children except when they hold POs or POAs. For most looked after children, local authorities have no PRRs and this affects day-to-day issues for children, such as medical consent and holiday arrangements. Local authorities do have duties (see Chapter 9) but not PRRs.

4.35

If a child is accommodated by the local authority, this is a voluntary arrangement with the consent of the parents and they do not lose PRRs. If they have any dispute with the local authority, they can ask for the child to be returned to them.

1995 Act, s.25

4.36

If a child is subject to a CSO in the hearing system, under ss.91 or 119 of the 2011 Act, the child may be at home or away from home. If the child is at home, the PRRs are only interfered with to the extent that the local authority have a responsibility to supervise. However, if a child is away from home on a CSO, the parents' PRRs will be interfered with to some extent. The parents' PRRs are effectively "suspended" in relation to control of residence and they cannot demand return of the child. The parents cannot act in any way which is incompatible with the CSO. When there is a CSO for a child, the courts cannot use s.11 to make orders about contact; only the Children's Hearing system can do this.

1995 Act, s.3(4) as amended by the Children's Hearings (Scotland) Act 2011 (Modification of Primary Legislation) Order 2013, SSI 2013/211; *P v P* 2000 SLT 781 (29 February 2000)

4.37
___

If someone wants to use s.11 to obtain a residence order for a child on a CSO, the court may grant such an order but the CSO still takes precedence. If the court grants an order to a carer named by the hearing system (e.g. a grandparent) then there is no conflict. If an order is granted to someone with whom the child does not live, it cannot be enforced unless and until the CSO is terminated or varied to name that person.

1995 Act, s.3(4) as amended; P v P 2000 SLT 781 (29 February 2000)

Section 62 referrals

4.38
___

Section 62 of the 2011 Act allows any civil court in a wide range of cases, including adoption, PO and POA applications, to refer a child to the children's reporter. The court specifies which s.67 grounds it thinks might apply. It is up to the reporter to decide whether to refer the child to a hearing. This is the way in which a court dealing with private law cases refers a child into the pubic law system if the court is concerned about the arrangements for the child (see Chapter 11 on the hearing system).

2011 Act, s.62

4.39
___

Courts no longer have powers to place a child directly into the care of the local authority or under supervision in private law cases, as they did before the 1995 Act came into force in 1996 and 1997.

1995 Act, Schedule 5

5

The 2010 Act and the Care Inspectorate

This chapter deals with the Public Services Reform (Scotland) Act 2010, which replaced part of the Regulation of Care (Scotland) Act 2001. The 2010 Act contains regulatory and inspection systems similar to those set up by the 2001 Act and replaced the Care Commission with the Care Inspectorate for many matters.

The 2001 and the 2010 Acts: the Care Inspectorate

5.1

The 2001 Act replaced the previous structures and systems for the registration of a wide range of care services in the health and social care sectors. It also established two new bodies – the Scottish Commission for the Regulation of Care (the Care Commission), and the Scottish Social Services Council (the Council). The 2001 Act remains in force for the Council.

5.2

Some of the services covered by the 2001 Act, like residential schools, childminding and nursing homes, were previously registered and inspected by local authorities prior to the 2001 Act coming into force. Other services, particularly adoption and fostering, were not registered and inspected at all, or only in a limited way. On 1 April 2002, the Care Commission took over existing local authority duties to register and inspect a range of services. The registration and inspection of other services was then introduced in stages, and all adoption and fostering services had to be registered with the Care Commission from 1 April 2004.

5.3

The 2010 Act covers a wide range of public authorities. From 1 April 2011, in relation to childcare and other matters, it dissolved the Care Commission and established two bodies in its place. They are: Social Care and Social Work Improvement Scotland (SCSWIS), otherwise the Care Inspectorate, and Health Improvement Scotland (HIS), to regulate health matters.

2010 Act, Part 5, ss.44 to 107 and Part 6, ss.108 to 110; see particularly ss.44, 52 and 108

5.4

The Care Inspectorate is now the body responsible for the regulation, registration and inspection of all the care services in Scotland listed in the 2010 Act. It deals with complaints about services and enforcement of Standards and conditions. The regulatory and inspection systems are similar to those under the 2001 Act. The Care Inspectorate also has a general duty to improve the quality of 'social services', which means 'care services' and 'social work services'. The latter are local authority and other social work services listed in Schedule 13.

2010 Act, Part 5, particularly ss.45 to 48, ss.50 and 51, and ss.53 to 92, and Schedules 12 and 13

5.5

There are 13 'care services' listed in s.47(1), with the detailed definitions set out in Schedule 12. They include support services, care home services, secure accommodation services, adoption services, fostering services, childminding and day care of children. Some of the services listed are only provided for children, like adoption, fostering and day care, but others are for all ages, such as care homes.

2010 Act, s.47 and Schedule 12

5.6

The Care Inspectorate took over from the Care Commission on 1 April 2011. All the care services listed now have to be registered with and inspected by the Care Inspectorate. For registration, there are general provisions for all care services except local authority adoption and fostering services. These are covered by other specific sections. There are general provisions about inspections of all care services.

2010 Act, ss.59 and 83 and ss.53 to 58.

5.7

There are a variety of regulations and orders made under the 2010 Act. These are not specific to one type of care service and include provisions for:

- commencement and transitional provisions;
- fees;
- registration of services; and
- requirements to be complied with by providers of care services.

There is information about them on the Care Inspectorate's website – see Further Reading.

5.8

As part of the system of registration and inspection, Scottish ministers are obliged to publish National Care Standards for the various care services. The Standards must be taken into account by the Care Inspectorate in all its decisions about registration, inspection and any proceedings under the 2010 Act. Despite the change in legislation from the 2001 to the 2010 Act, the existing Standards remain in place.

2010 Act, s.50

5.9
—

The main National Care Standards for services for or including children are:

- Adoption Standards – see Chapter 13;

- Care at home;

- Care homes for children and young people;

- Childcare agencies – see Chapter 6;

- Early education and childcare up to the age of 16 – see Chapter 6;

- Fostering Standards – see Chapter 10;

- School care accommodation services.

The Standards are available through the Care Commission's website – see Further Reading.

The Scottish Social Services Council

5.10
—

The Council is responsible for the registration in Scotland of people who work in social services, and for regulating their education and training. The Register of Social Service Workers in Scotland opened on 1 April 2003 for all workers with a Diploma in Social Work (DipSW) or equivalent qualification. Qualified social workers had to register by 1 May 2005 in order to meet the deadline for protection of the title of "social worker", which came into effect on 1 September 2005.

2001 Act, s.44 and 52

5.11
—

The Council must also promote high standards of behaviour and practice among social services workers and in education and training. There are UK-wide Codes developed by the Council and the equivalent regulatory bodies in the rest of the UK. These lay down the standards of conduct and practice that people can expect from social service workers and their employers. All workers and employers are expected to adhere to the Codes.

2001 Act, s.43 and 53

6

Private arrangements

This chapter deals with private care arrangements which parents and families may make for their children at home, or with relatives or with other people. Childminding and day care of children were formerly covered by the 1989 Act, then the 2001 Act, and are now regulated by the 2010 Act.

Arrangements at home

6.1
——

If parents make arrangements directly with a carer for babysitting or childcare in their own home, *without* the involvement of a child care agency, there are no controls over these. The 2010 Act does not cover such arrangements. However, a carer and/or the parents could be liable criminally if the arrangements are inadequate.

1937 Act, s. 12

6.2
——

When carers for children do not have parental responsibilities and rights (PRRs), they still have a general duty to safeguard the children's welfare. Carers may also be able to consent to medical treatment in certain circumstances: carers must be at least 16, the children must be unable to consent and the carers should have no reason to believe that the parents would refuse to consent.

1995 Act, s.5

6.3

It is not an offence to leave children under 16 unattended, but if harm or neglect is suffered by the children, the people who left them unattended may be charged with a criminal offence. This applies to parents and any other carers who are 16 or over.

1937 Act, s.12

Arrangements with family

6.4

If parents make arrangements for a child to be cared for by a close relative, there is no regulatory control or involvement. If the relative is not a close one and the care is for less than 28 days, there is still no regulatory control. If the care is for more than 28 days, then it will be a private fostering arrangement and the local authority must be notified. See Chapter 10, paragraphs 10.11 to 10.19.

Childminding

6.5

Childminding was formerly regulated under the 1989 Act, and then under the 2001 Act. It is now one of the care services listed in the 2010 Act. Childminders must therefore register with the Care Inspectorate (see Chapter 5). There are conditions in regulations for registration and it may be refused. There is an annual registration and inspection fee. In addition, the Care Inspectorate must inspect the premises which are used for childminding and the arrangements.

2010 Act, s.47 and Schedule 12, paragraphs 12 and 14, s.59 and Part 5 generally

6.6

Childminding means 'looking after one or more children on domestic premises for reward'. It is not childminding when a child is cared for by a parent, relative, someone with parental responsibilities and rights or a public or private foster carer; or if the care is provided by anyone for less than two hours in each day; or if the child is cared for mainly in the parents' home or the home of other parents, when the care is shared.

2010 Act, Schedule 12, paragraphs 12 and 14

6.7

The Standards which apply to childminding are the *National Care Standards: Early education and childcare up to the age of 16.*

6.8

A nanny is not a childminder if she or he is looking after a child in the home of her or his employer. However, if he or she has been supplied or introduced to the parents by a child care agency, that is a child care agency service, which is regulated by the 2001 Act. See paragraphs 6.11 and 6.12 below.

2001 Act, Schedule 12, paragraphs 12(3) and 5

Day care

6.9

Day care was formerly regulated under 1989 Act and then under the 2001 Act. It is now a care service in the 2010 Act. It is defined in the 2010 Act as a service providing:

> any form of care (whether or not provided to any extent in the form of an educational activity), supervised by a responsible person and not excepted from this definition by regulations, provided for children, on premises other than domestic premises, during the day (whether or not it is provided on a regular basis or commences or ends during the hours of daylight).

Providers must register with the Care Inspectorate, which may impose certain conditions. These include specifying the number of children able to be cared for and the number of helpers. Registration may be refused or cancelled. The Care Inspectorate must inspect day services.

2010 Act, s.47 and Schedule 12, paragraphs 13 to 18, s.59 and Part 5 generally

6.10

Day care can include nursery classes, crèches, after-school groups and playgroups. They may be run by the public, private or voluntary sectors. The Standards are the *National Care Standards: Early education and childcare up to the age of 16*.

Child care agencies

6.11

Child care agencies are a care service defined originally in the 2001 Act and now in the 2010 Act. They are services 'supplying, or introducing to persons who use the service, child carers' to look after children up to the age of 16, wholly or mainly in their homes, and 'whether or not for reward and whether on a day-to-day or on an occasional basis'. They may include nanny agencies, home-based child care services and sitter services. The agencies may be managed by private, voluntary or local authority providers.

2010 Act, Schedule 12, paragraph 5

6.12

The supply or introduction of child carers through a child care agency was previously regulated under the 2001 Act and the provisions about them came into force on 1 April 2003. The provisions of the 2010 Act now apply instead, from 1 April 2011. Agencies must register with the Care Inspectorate, which may impose certain conditions. Registration may be refused or cancelled. The Care Inspectorate must inspect child care agencies. The Standards are the *National Care Standards: Childcare agencies.*

2010 Act, s.47 and Schedule 12, paragraph 5, s.59 and Part 5 generally

6.13

When parents enter into arrangements directly with a child carer for babysitting or child care in their home, without involving an agency, the arrangements are not subject to regulation under the 2010 Act. See paragraph 6.1 above.

Private fostering

6.14

Private fostering is care of a child provided:

- by an individual who is *not* a close relative; and

- on a private basis by arrangement between the parents and the individual; and

- for a period of 28 days or more.

Private fostering is covered by the 1984 Act and the 1985 Regs. It must be distinguished from public foster care arranged by the local authority, where the local authority make such arrangements and place a child with approved foster carers. Public fostering makes a child a 'looked after' child. Public and private fostering are both dealt with in Chapter 10.

1984 Act; 1985 Regs

7

General local authority duties to children

This chapter deals with the general duties of local authorities to all children in their area, and in particular towards children 'in need'. These provisions are concerned with what is generally seen as preventive work. Local authority duties to 'looked after' children are dealt with in Chapter 9.

7.1

The duties in this chapter and which are in the 1995 Act are on the whole local authority duties and not just to the social work department – see Chapter 2, paragraph 2.14.

1995 Act, s.93(1)

General welfare duty

7.2

Local authorities are under a statutory duty to promote social welfare generally for all people in their area, by giving advice, guidance and assistance. Under these provisions, they may give assistance in kind to children and families, and in cash and kind to those over 18, although there are some restrictions under the immigration legislation.

1968 Act, s.12 as amended by the 1995 Act, Schedule 4, para 15(11)

Children's Services Plans and Adoption Services Plans

7.3

Local authorities are obliged to produce a Children's Services Plan for their area covering all the 'relevant services' they have to provide for children. These are not only the duties, powers and services under the 1995 Act, but also other ones in a range of legislation, including, for example, the Mental Health (Care and Treatment) (Scotland) Act 2003.

1995 Act, s.19, which refers to the list in s.5(1B) of the 1968 Act

7.4

When Children's Services Plans were introduced under the 1995 Act, the range of services to be covered included local authorities' adoption provision. However, the 2007 Act introduced a specific duty on local authorities to prepare plans about the adoption services they provide in their areas. These adoption plans may be prepared separately from overall Children's Services Plans or included in them.

2007 Act, s.4

7.5

The 2014 Act introduces a new scheme of children's services planning, which will repeal and replace s.19 of the 1995 Act and s.4 of the 2007 Act, when it comes into force. The proposed new scheme covers a similar range of children's services and also places duties about service planning on a range of other authorities.

2014 Act, Part 3, ss.7 to 18

Children 'in need'

7.6

The 1995 Act introduced a definition of children in need as being children for whom as wide a range as possible of services should be provided, to promote their welfare and to assist them to develop. The main provision is in s.22 of the 1995 Act, but that section did not replace the general duty to do preventive work in s.12 of the 1968 Act.

1995 Act, s.22

7.7

In practice, local authorities use their powers under s.22 to provide services to children in need, and may also use s.12 of the 1968 Act as well.

7.8

Local authorities must safeguard and promote the welfare of children in their area who are in need. The services provided under this duty may be for:

- the child; or
- his or her family, if the services help the child; or
- any other member of the family, if the services help the child.

These services may be in cash or kind.

1995 Act, s.22(1) and (3)

7.9

The definition of in need is very wide, and each local authority must have instructions and guidance so that individual decisions can be made about children and families. A child will be considered in need if he or she is:

- unlikely to achieve or maintain or have the opportunity of achieving or maintaining a reasonable standard of health or development unless he or she receives services; or
- his or her health or development is likely significantly to be impaired or further impaired unless services are provided; or

- he or she is disabled; or

- he or she is adversely affected by the disability of any other person in the family.

1995 Act, s.93(4)(a)

Disabled children and children affected by disability

7.10

The definition of in need means that children who are adversely affected by the disability of someone else in the family are covered, as well as children who are themselves disabled. This includes children who act as carers for others in the family. The duties about carers' assessments (see paragraph 7.13 below) apply to child carers as well as to adult ones.

1995 Act, s.24 as amended by the Community Care and Health (Scotland) Act 2002, s.11(1)

7.11

Disability is defined as 'chronically sick or disabled or [having] a mental disorder (as defined in section 328(1) of the Mental Health (Care and Treatment) (Scotland) Act 2003)'.

1995 Act, s.23(2) as amended by the 2003 Act, Schedule 4, para 7

7.12

When a child is in need because of disability, the parents may ask for an assessment of the child or anyone else in the family, to establish the child's needs so far as attributable to the disability. The local authority must carry out this assessment if it is requested. They must take account of the views of the child, the parents and any carer who is providing 'substantial' care to the disabled person; and take account of the 'substantial' care when that is provided.

1995 Act, s.23(3) and (4), the latter inserted by the Community Care and Health (Scotland) Act 2002, s.10

7.13

Anyone providing substantial care for a disabled child (including another child) can also ask for a carer's assessment of his or her ability to provide the care. The local authority must carry out this assessment if they consider that the child should or may receive services as a child in need. When a child is in need because he or she is disabled, and the carer is providing substantial care, the local authority must tell him or her about being entitled to a carer's assessment.

1995 Act, s.24(1) and (1A), and s.24A, inserted by the Community Care and Health (Scotland) Act 2002, s.11

Day care for children in need

7.14

When a child is in need, the local authority have a duty to provide day care for that child:

● during the day if the child is under five; *or*

● after school *and* during holidays if the child is attending school.

See Chapter 6 for general arrangements about day care. Local authorities also have discretion to provide these services for other children in their area who are not in need.

1995 Act, s.27

7.15

When the 2014 Act is in force, it amends s.27 and imposes further duties on local authorities. At least every two years, they must consult "representative" parents of children in need and children not in need, about how these services should be provided. They must then publish their plans for delivery of these services.

1995 Act, s.27 as amended by the 2014 Act, s.55

2014 Act

7.16

When it is in force, the 2014 Act has a number of provisions which affect local authorities' duties and powers to children in their area. Some of these apply to all children, some to children in need, and some to children who are likely to be looked after or are looked after or have been looked after.

Early learning and child care

7.17

The 2014 Act imposes a duty on every 'education authority', (i.e. a local authority's education service), to provide 'early learning and childcare' for 'each eligible pre-school child' in their area. A child will be 'eligible' if he or she:

- is under school age, *and*
- has not started ordinary primary school, *and*
  - is aged 2 or over and is looked after (see Chapter 9), *or*
  - is aged 2 or over and is the subject of a kinship care order (see Chapter 10, paragraph 10.25), *or*
  - is otherwise specified in secondary legislation.

An education authority may provide alternative arrangements for an 'eligible' looked after child in certain situations.

2014 Act, ss.68 to 70

Children at risk of being looked after

7.18

The 2014 Act also requires every local authority to provide 'relevant services' for children in their area who are at risk of being looked after or otherwise fit other descriptions in secondary legislation. Services involve providing information, advice, counselling or taking other actions, which may include payments. The duties extend to parents of such children and to pregnant women and their partners when expected children are likely to be looked after.

2014 Act, ss.68 to 70

Wellbeing duties

7.19

The 2014 Act amends the 1995 Act by inserting a new s.23A. This imposes a duty on local authorities when carrying out their duties towards children who are:

- in need (see paragraphs 7.6 to 7.9), or
- looked after (see Chapter 9), or
- receiving continuing care (see Chapter 9, paragraph 9.13).

Local authorities must carry out their duties to and provide services for children in such a way as to 'safeguard, support and promote their [children's] wellbeing'. Wellbeing is defined in s.96 of the 2014 Act. This lists the eight indicators of wellbeing used in the 'Getting it right for every child' (GIRFEC) policies. These indicators are referred to by the acronym SHANARRI – Safe, Healthy, Achieving, Nurtured, Active, Respected, Responsible and Included.

1995 Act, s.23A, inserted by the 2014 Act, s.95; 2014 Act, s.96

Named person service

7.20

The 'named person service' is not a really a general local authority duty – see paragraph 7.21 – but it is convenient to cover it here. Under the 2014 Act, every child should have a named person. The concept of named persons was developed as part of the GIRFEC policies and has operated in some areas such as Highland for a number of years. Each child has a 'named person' whose function is to provide advice, information and support for the child or parent, *or* help them access services and support *or* to discuss or raise 'a matter about the child' with service providers or a 'relevant authority' such as social or education services.

2014 Act, ss.19 to 32

7.21

The named person service for pre-school children is provided by the health board for the area where they live. For other children, with a few exceptions, the service is provided by the local authority where they live. There are provisions about information sharing in relation to children. The Scottish Government may issue guidance.

2014 Act, ss. 20 and 21 and ss.26 to 28

8

Child protection

This chapter briefly outlines the child protection system and the three court orders used for the purposes of child protection, in the 1995 and 2011 Acts.

Child protection

8.1

Most of the child protection system is organised on the basis of Guidance from the Scottish Government and is not contained in statutes. The Guidance requires there to be local Child Protection Committees with inter-disciplinary membership, and local child protection policies and guidelines. These cover such matters as what the different agencies should do when they have concerns about children, child protection case conferences, and when children should be "registered" on the local Child Protection Register. Social work departments and the police are expected to be the lead agencies and all agencies should work co-operatively.

2010 National Child Protection Guidance, as amended

8.2

When local authorities have emergency concerns about a child, they should consider the use of the various court orders available under the 1995 and 2011 Acts – see below. They may also, as may any agency or person, refer a child to the children's reporter. If a local authority or the police think that a child may need compulsory measures of supervision, they must refer to the reporter. See Chapter 11, paragraphs 11.8 to 11.10.

Child Assessment Orders (CAOs)

8.3

This order was a new introduction to the law of Scotland in the 1995 Act. It has now been moved to the 2011 Act. It allows local authorities (and only local authorities) to apply to the sheriff to grant an order for an assessment of:

> *(a) the child's health or development, or*

> *(b) the way in which the child has been or is being treated or neglected.*

The sheriff has to be satisfied that:

> *(a) the local authority have reasonable cause to suspect –*

>> *(i) that the child has been or is being treated in such a way that the child is suffering or is likely to suffer significant harm, or*

>> *(ii) that the child has been or is being neglected and as a result of the neglect the child is suffering or is likely to suffer significant harm,*

> [and]

> *(b) an assessment [of the type mentioned above] is necessary in order to establish whether there is reasonable cause to believe that the child has been or is being so treated or neglected, and*

> *(c) it is unlikely that the assessment could be carried out, or carried out satisfactorily, unless the order was made.*

2011 Act, ss.35 and 36

8.4

The order can last for a maximum of three days and must specify the period for which it has effect. It can authorise the production of the child to anyone for the purposes of assessment, and taking the child to any place for the assessment. It can allow any type of assessment. One obvious use is for medical assessment, but the order is not restricted to that.

2011 Act, s.35

8.5
___

There are no regulations regarding these orders and the child is not looked after by the local authority.

8.6
___

There are court rules about applying for CAOs. Notice is given to the child's family, as ordered by the sheriff. CAOs may, however, be obtained on fairly short notice. If parents wish to oppose an application for an order, they appear before the sheriff, who hears both sides of the application.

AS 1997, r.3.13(2) and rr.3.25 to 3.28, and general provisions, rr.3.1 to 3.24, all as amended for the 2011 Act

8.7
___

When a CAO application is made, a sheriff may grant a CPO instead of a CAO, if he or she thinks that the conditions for a CPO are satisfied.

2011 Act, s.36(3)

Child Protection Orders (CPOs)

8.8
___

Under the 1995 Act, this order replaced the "place of safety" formerly obtained under s.37 of the 1968 Act. It was therefore not a new remedy, but the procedures were different from those under the 1968 Act. It has now been moved to the 2011 Act.

2011 Act, ss.37 to 54

8.9
___

Anyone may apply for a CPO, including local authorities. Almost all applications are by local authorities. All applications must go to the sheriff. There are two different tests depending on who is applying.

8.10

If an application is made by "any person" (including the local authority), the sheriff may grant the order if satisfied that –

   (a) *there are reasonable grounds to believe that –*

   (i) *the child has been or is being treated in such a way that the child is suffering or is likely to suffer significant harm,* [or]

   (ii) *the child has been or is being neglected and as a result of the neglect the child is suffering or is likely to suffer significant harm,* [or]

   (iii) *the child is likely to suffer significant harm if the child is not removed to and kept in a place of safety, or*

   (iv) *the child is likely to suffer significant harm if the child does not remain in the place at which the child is staying (whether or not the child is resident there), and*

   (b) *the order is necessary to protect the child from that harm or from further harm.*

2011 Act, s.39

8.11

If an application is made by a local authority, they may either satisfy the above test or the one in s.38. The sheriff may grant the order if satisfied that –

   (a) *the local authority has reasonable grounds to suspect that –*

   (i) *the child has been or is being treated in such a way that the child is suffering or is likely to suffer significant harm,* [or]

   (ii) *the child has been or is being neglected and as a result of the neglect the child is suffering or is likely to suffer significant harm, or*

   (iii) *the child will be treated or neglected in such a way that is likely to cause significant harm to the child,* [and]

(b) the local authority is making enquiries to allow it to decide whether to take action to safeguard the welfare of the child, or is causing those enquiries to be made, [and]

(c) those enquiries are being frustrated by access to the child being unreasonably denied, and

(d) the local authority has reasonable cause to believe that access is required as a matter of urgency.

2011 Act, s.38

8.12
___
A local authority may use either test, but anyone else can only use the test in paragraph 8.10.

8.13
___
Again, there are court rules about applying for CPOs. They are dealt with on an emergency basis and it is not mandatory to give advance notice to the family, although some sheriffs require this in some cases. If the sheriff is satisfied and grants an order, the local authority or other applicant must immediately serve on or give to the family a copy of the order. This should be done when they remove the child or tell the family that the child is not being removed from the place of safety where he or she already is. A copy of the order will also be sent to the child, unless the sheriff decides this is not appropriate, given the child's age and maturity.

AS 1997, rr.3.29 to 3.33, and general provisions, rr.3.1 to 3.24, all as amended for the 2011 Act

8.14
___
If a CPO is granted, the child does not become a looked after child (see Chapter 9). However, if the child is removed to a place of safety under the order, the local authority has the same duties to him or her as if she is looked after. Also, the child must be referred immediately to the children's reporter,

who must decide whether he or she will take the case forward to a children's hearing. There are complicated rules about times within which hearings must be held, and failure to stick to the rules means that the CPO will fall. Decisions about whether the child continues to be subject to the CPO are made by the children's hearing members and/or the sheriff, depending on whether the family exercises its rights to ask the sheriff to reconsider the case. A CPO lasts for a maximum of eight working days. At the end of that time, if the case is proceeding, there must be a hearing at which s.67 grounds for referral are put and a decision made as to whether the child is to continue to be "away from home" on an interim CSO (see Chapter 11).

2011 Act, ss.43 to 54

Emergency protection

8.15

There are arrangements for sheriffs to be available for CPO applications to be heard at any time, including out of hours. If, however, a local authority or other persons are unable to present an application to a sheriff, they may seek emergency protection from a Justice of the Peace. The Justice has to be satisfied on the same terms as the sheriff, and also 'that it is not practicable in the circumstances' for a sheriff to deal with the matter. If such emergency protection is obtained, it falls after 12 hours if not implemented. In any case, it may only last for a maximum of 24 hours, by which time the matter must be put before a sheriff with a CPO application, unless the child goes home.

2011 Act, s.55

8.16

The police have a similar power to give emergency protection for up to 24 hours.

2011 Act, s.56

Exclusion Orders (EOs)

8.17

Like CPOs and CAOs, EOs were introduced by the 1995 Act and represented a new remedy. They have not been moved to the 2011 Act and remain in the 1995 Act. They allow a person to be removed from the family home if the child is at risk, as an alternative to removing the child from home. Only a local authority may apply and the application must be made to a sheriff.

8.18

The sheriff must be satisfied that:

- the child has suffered, is suffering or is likely to suffer 'significant harm' because of the behaviour, threats, etc, of the 'named person'; *and*

- that it is necessary to make an EO against the 'named person' to protect the child, this being a better safeguard for the child than taking him or her away from home; *and*

- that if the order is made, there will be an 'appropriate person' in the house to care for the child and anyone else there.

1995 Act, s.76(2)

8.19

Again, there are court rules about these applications. An application for an EO may either be on an "emergency basis", without notice, or be heard after notice has been given to the family and to the 'named person'.

AS 1997, rr.3.34 to 3.40

8.20

A sheriff may grant an interim EO without giving notice to the 'named person', but it may be difficult to satisfy a sheriff that this should be done.

1995 Act, s.76(4)

8.21

Another practical difficulty is that the local authority, in applying for the order, and the sheriff, in granting it, have to be satisfied that there is an 'appropriate person' and that he or she will fully protect the child and anyone else in the house, and not simply allow the 'named person' back into the house.

1995 Act, s.76(2)(c)

8.22

An EO can last for a maximum of six months. When the sheriff initially grants the order it will probably be as an interim order, whether notice has been given or not. An interim order is as good as a full order, unless it has been granted on an emergency basis. In that case, there must be another hearing within three days, after notice to the 'named person'. Conditions and powers of arrest may be attached to an EO or interim EO after notice.

1995 Act, s. 79, s.77 and s.78; AS 1997, r.3.36

8.23

When an application is made for an EO, the sheriff may grant a CPO instead of the EO if satisfied that the conditions for a CPO are met.

1995 Act, s.76(8), as amended by the 2011 Act, Schedule 5, paragraph 2(9)

The Disclosure system

8.24

The system of making criminal record checks is a useful tool in child (and adult) protection. There is information about the system in Chapter 2, paragraphs 2.15 to 2.20.

9

Local authority responsibilities for 'looked after' children

This chapter deals with looked after children, who they are, and what responsibilities local authorities have.

'Looked after' children

9.1
___

Looked after children is the term which was introduced by the 1995 Act and replaced references to children "in care". The definition of looked after child is wider than the various definitions of in care and is different from the definitions in the law for England and Wales.

Who are looked after children?

9.2
___

The definition of a looked after child is in s.17(6) of the 1995 Act, as amended by and under the 2007 and 2011 Acts. Children are looked after if they are:

- accommodated by a local authority under s.25 of the 1995 Act, that is, accommodated on a voluntary basis;

- subject to compulsory supervision orders, CSOs or interim CSOs made by children's hearings under the 2011 Act (see Chapter 11);

- living in Scotland and subject to orders giving Scottish local authorities responsibilities, after transfers of orders under the

- Children (Reciprocal Enforcement of Prescribed Orders etc (England and Wales and Northern Ireland) (Scotland) Regulations 1996, SI 1996/3267, made under s.33 of the 1995 Act; or

- Children's Hearings (Scotland) Act 2011 (Transfer of Children to Scotland – Effect of Orders made in England and Wales or Northern Ireland) Regulations 2013, SSI 2013/99, made under s.190 of the 2011 Act;

- subject to POs and POAs made under s.80 of the 2007 Act, including deemed POs, which were formerly parental responsibilities orders (PROs) under s.86 of the 1995 Act.

In practical terms, children may be looked after in many different ways, including at home, in foster care, in kinship care, with prospective adopters, in residential placements and in secure accommodation.

1995 Act, s.17(6) (as amended by the 2007 and 2011 Acts), s.25 and s.33; 2007 Act, s.80; 2011 Act, s.91, s.119 and s.190

9.3

This is a definitive list. If the authority for the placement or keeping of a child is not in this list, the child is not looked after. The list *does not* include a child who:

- is accommodated by virtue purely of educational placements; *or*

- is accommodated in a refuge provided under s.38 of the 1995 Act; *or*

- is the subject of a CAO, CPO or EO.

However, when a child is the subject of a CPO requiring the child to be removed to a place of safety, the local authority have the same duties towards the child as if he or she is looked after.

1995 Act, s.17(6) as amended; 2011 Act, s.44

Duties of the local authority

9.4

There are a wide variety of duties owed by the local authority to looked after children. These duties are contained in the 1995 Act and the various regulations made thereunder, particularly the LAC Regulations 2009 and the Leaving Care Regs 2003. The Guidance to the 2007 Act is also important.

1995 Act, ss.17 and 29 to 31, as amended and added to by the 2014 Act; LAC Regs 2009; Leaving Care Regs 2003; 2007 Act Guidance

9.5

The local authority duties listed in the 1995 Act are amended by the 2014 Act when it is in force. The duties are to:

- safeguard and promote the child's welfare as paramount concern;

- safeguard, support and protect the child's wellbeing (inserted by the 2014 Act when it is in force – see paragraph 9.13);

- make such use of services for the children as reasonable parents would;

- promote regular personal relations and direct contact between the child and anyone with parental responsibilities, *having regard to* the child's welfare as paramount *and* what is practical and appropriate;

- provide advice and assistance to a child, with a view to preparing him or her for when he or she is no longer looked after;

- find out and take account of the views of the child, his or her parents and others with responsibilities and rights or an interest in the child, before making any decisions about the child;

- take account of the child's religious persuasion, racial origin and cultural and linguistic background before making any decisions;

- carry out a review of each child's case at set intervals; and

- provide advice, guidance and assistance to any child who was looked after at the date on which he or she could leave school, is no longer looked after by a local authority and is under 19 – these duties are changed by the 2014 Act – see paragraphs 9.12 and 9.13.

1995 Act, s.17(1) to (4), s.23A, s.31, s.29 as amended by the 2001 and 2014 Acts and s.29A

9.6

Further details of these and other duties are contained in the LAC Regs 2009 referred to above. There are some differences in the provisions as between children who are looked after and remain at home with their parents and those who are looked after away from their parents, with foster carers, kinship carers, in residential placements or with carers who have some PRRs under a PO or POA. The LAC Regs 2009 cover a range of matters, including:

- what information has to be gathered and assessments made before or when children are looked after;

- that before or when children become looked after, there must be a written assessment of their health and need for health care;

- what requires to be in children's plans for all looked after children;

- notification of the death of looked after children;

- arrangements for different types of care for looked after children;

- notifications of placements;

- emergency placement arrangements;

- how and when children's cases are to be reviewed; and

- maintenance of case records for looked after children.

LAC Regs 2009, regs.1 to 14, regs.27 to 30; regs.34 to 49

9.7

The provisions about reviews in the LAC Regulations 2009 are in two separate regulations for two different groups of looked after children. Regulation

44 covers children looked after and cared for by their parents or by other people who have parental responsibilities and rights (PRRs). This will include carers who have PRRs under POs or POAs. Regulation 45 covers children looked after and "placed" with kinship carers, foster carers, emergency carers (reg.39(1)) or residential establishments. Regulation 45 includes children who have "respite" placements – see paragraph 9.11. However, neither regulation mentions children who are looked after under CSOs or interim CSOs which name carers who are not parents, have no PRRs and are not approved kinship or foster carers. For these children, reg.45 should be used, as reg.44 clearly does not apply.

LAC Regs 2009, regs.44 and 45

9.8

Under reg.44, the frequency of reviews is not fixed automatically. The local authority have to discuss how often reviews will be held with individual children (depending on age and maturity) and carers. If there is no agreement about frequency, there must be a review within six weeks of placement, and at least every 12 months thereafter.

LAC Regs 2009, reg.44

9.9

Under reg.45 there is a fixed structure of timescales for reviews, with some slight differences, depending on how children came into the care system and are looked after. Reviews for most children must be within six weeks of the placement; then within a further three months; and then within every six months thereafter. Children who are looked after because respite care is provided only need to have reviews three months after the first placement, and then within every six months thereafter.

LAC Regs 2009, reg.45

Provision of accommodation

9.10

Local authorities have a duty to accommodate children for whom no one has parental responsibilities, or who are lost or abandoned, or who cannot be cared for by their normal carers, temporarily or permanently, for whatever reason. Such care is often referred to as "voluntary" care, as it comes about by agreement with parents or carers, or a complete absence of any parents or carers, not because of an order from a court or a hearing. The local authority must provide such accommodation for children up to 18 where they fall into the above categories. Children accommodated in this way are looked after and placed.

1995 Act, s.25

Respite care

9.11

This term is not specifically mentioned in the 1995 Act or the LAC Regs 2009, but the effect of these is that all respite placements which are planned by local authorities and which last for more than 24 hours at a time are treated as looked after placements in terms of s.25 (provision of accommodation – see paragraph 9.10). Such arrangements are therefore regulated and the children are treated as looked after and placed children. This includes children with disabilities for whom such respite care is provided. If respite is provided in family homes as opposed to residential establishments, the carers must be foster carers or kinship carers approved in terms of the LAC Regs 2009 – see Chapter 10 about foster carer and kinship carer approval. A series of "respite" placements are treated as a single placement. The first review must be within three months of the first placement; and only one medical assessment is needed at the beginning, not every time a child receives "respite" care.

LAC Regs 2009, reg.14 (kinship care) and reg.30 (foster care) and reg.45(3)

Throughcare, aftercare and continuing care

9.12

Local authorities have "throughcare and aftercare" duties to certain young people when they cease to be looked after. When the young people cease to be looked after at or after the age they could leave school (i.e. 15½ to 16½), and whether or not they do leave school, local authorities have duties under s.29 of the 1995 Act as amended by the 2001 Act and the Leaving Care Regulations 2003. They must assess the needs of eligible young people and provide support until such young people are 19 and may do so until they are 21.

1995 Act, s.29 as amended; Leaving Care Regs 2003; Leaving Care Guidance 2004

9.13

When it is in force, the 2014 Act changes the aftercare system. It provides that:

- the qualifying age for aftercare is 16;
- local authorities have the power to provide aftercare for formerly looked after young people, up to the age of 26; and
- local authorities have a duty to provide 'continuing care' for formerly looked after young people, from the age of 16, allowing them to remain living in their accommodation even although they are no longer looked after.

The 'continuing care' system is expected to be in force from April 2015, with an upper age limit of 21. Local authorities must have regard to their wellbeing duties when they are providing continuing care – see Chapter 7, paragraph 7.19.

2014 Act, s.66 amending the 1995 Act, s.29, and ss.67 and 95 inserting new sections, s.26A and 23A; 2014 Act s.96

10

Fostering and kinship care

This chapter briefly outlines the law about fostering, including the different types of fostering, and kinship care.

Types of fostering

10.1

There are basically two types of fostering:

- public fostering, governed by the 1995 Act and the LAC Regs 2009; and

- private fostering, governed by the 1984 Act and the 1985 Regs.

1995 Act; LAC Regs 2009; 1984 Act; 1985 Regs

10.2

The 2010 Act lists fostering as one of the care services which must be registered and inspected. Schedule 12, paragraph 9 sets out what makes up fostering services and paragraph 10 says what they can be described as.

- The 'Scottish public fostering service' is the service mentioned in paragraph 9(a) and (b). This is a local authority's own direct service provision under s.26(1) of the 1995 Act *and* their arrangements with voluntary organisations, otherwise called registered fostering services (RFS). Both of these services are for children 'looked after' by authorities in terms of the 1995 Act.

- The 'Scottish private fostering service' is the service mentioned in paragraph 9(c). This is the range of duties which local authorities have under the 1984 Act.

2010 Act, ss.59 and 83 and Schedule 12, paragraphs 9 and 10; 1995 Act; 1984 Act

10.3

There is confusion about the differences between the two types of fostering, and particularly about how private fostering works. There are no reliable statistics about how many private fostering arrangements exist in Scotland.

10.4

Both fostering services are regulated and covered by the 2010 Act. From 1 April 2004, all public fostering services run by local authorities and by voluntary organisations had to be registered with and inspected by the Care Commission. In addition, local authorities' private fostering services, their duties under the 1984 Act and 1985 Regs, had to be registered with and inspected by the Care Commission from that date. These requirements are now contained in the 2010 Act and the services have been registered with and inspected by the Care Inspectorate from 1 April 2011. See Chapter 5 for more information on the 2010 Act and the Care Inspectorate.

2010 Act, ss.59 and 83 and Schedule 12, paragraphs 9 and 10

Public fostering

10.5

Public fostering is where children are looked after by local authorities and placed in family homes with approved foster carers. The children may be looked after in one of a variety of ways – see Chapter 9, paragraph 9.2. All fostered children are looked after and are therefore covered by the local authority duties set out in the LAC Regulations 2009. The same regulations also cover all aspects of foster carers' assessment, approval, etc, and placement of children in foster care.

1995 Act, s.25 and s.26; LAC Regs 2009, including regs.17 to 33 and regs.48 and 49 and Schedules 3, 4 and 6

10.6

The LAC Regs 2009 cover:

- the establishment of fostering panels;
- the assessment and approval of foster carers;
- reviews of foster carers' approval;
- placements in foster care and notifications of them;
- short-term placements – respite care;
- case records for foster carers;
- fostering allowances; and
- arrangements between local authorities and RFSs.

There are also Schedules which set out the information which should be obtained on the prospective foster carers when they are assessed; matters to be covered in individual Foster Carer Agreements, i.e. contracts between foster carers and the authority or RFS which approved them; and matters to be covered in individual Foster Placement Agreements about each child placed.

LAC Regs 2009

10.7

All foster carers must be assessed and approved by local authorities or RFSs. Local authorities can place children with carers approved by other authorities or by RFSs. All local authorities and RFSs have a fostering panel. These panels make recommendations on the approval, etc, of carers.

LAC Regs 2009, regs.17 to 20 and reg.48

10.8

Public foster carers do not acquire parental responsibilities and rights (PRRs) simply because of fostering placements. Carers have general duties and rights in relation to the children in their care under s.5 of the 1995 Act, and may be able to consent to medical treatment – see Chapter 6, paragraph 6.2. Foster carers who look after children who are subject to compulsory supervision orders (CSOs) and interim CSOs may be 'deemed' relevant persons for the purposes of the hearing system – see Chapter 11, paragraphs 11.16 to 11.18. Foster carers who look after children under POs or POAs may have some PRRs for them, depending on the terms of the individual order – see Chapter 12, particularly paragraphs 12.5 to 12.7 and 12.31.

1995 Act, s.5; 2011 Act, s.81; 2007 Act, ss.80 and 82

10.9

Registered fostering services (RFSs) assess and approve foster carers in the same way as local authorities. A RFS must be a voluntary organisation, which is defined as 'a body, other than a public or local authority, the activities of which are not carried on for profit'. Before a RFS may provide foster carers to a local authority, it must make formal arrangements with the authority, under reg.48 of the LAC Regs 2009, as amended.

2010 Act, s.59(3) and s.105(1); LAC Regs 2009, reg.2 as amended for the 2010 Act, reg.48 as amended and Schedule 7

10.10

Local authorities and RFSs must take account of the Fostering Standards and are inspected against them.

2010 Act, s.50

Private fostering

10.11

Private fostering is care provided on a private basis by arrangement between parents and someone who is *not* a close relative. As explained above, it is to be distinguished from public foster care arranged by the local authority.

10.12

Separate legislation covers private fostering arrangements. Arrangements are private fostering ones when:

● the arrangements are made by someone who has parental responsibilities and rights for the child;

● the child is placed with someone who is not a close relative or guardian;

● the child is under the compulsory school leaving age; and

● the care arrangements are for 28 days or more.

1984 Act, s.1 and s.2

10.13

A "relative" is defined in the 1984 Act as grandparents, brothers and sisters, uncles and aunts, whether full or half blood or by affinity (relationship through marriage or civil partnership). So if more distant relatives care for a child for more than 28 days, that is a private fostering arrangement.

1984 Act, s.21

10.14

Where such private arrangements are made, the parent and carer must notify the local authority not less than two weeks before the arrangement starts, unless it is an emergency. In the case of an emergency, notification must be made within one week.

1984 Act, s.4 and s.5; 1985 Regs

10.15

When the local authority are notified, they have a duty to be satisfied about the well-being of the child. The child must be visited within one week of the placement and on a regular basis thereafter. The authority may prohibit such private arrangements, or impose conditions on the arrangements if they are not satisfied.

1984 Act, s.3, s.9 and s.10; 1985 Regs

10.16

Some people may be disqualified from being private foster carers, including those convicted of certain criminal offences and/or those who have been refused registration or removed from registration as childminders.

1984 Act, s.7

10.17

Private foster carers who are caring for children do not have parental responsibilities and rights (PRRs). They have general rights of control because they are acting in the place of parents. They must usually return the child to his or her parents on request unless they have obtained some other authority to keep the child.

10.18

Private foster carers have a general obligation to safeguard and protect the child's welfare and the right to consent to medical treatment in certain circumstances – see Chapter 6, paragraph 6.2.

1995 Act, s.5

10.19

Although local authorities' private fostering services must be registered with and inspected by the Care Inspectorate (see paragraph 10.4), there are no

National Care Standards for private fostering. However, Scottish Government Guidance was issued in 2013.

Private Fostering Guidance

Kinship care

10.20

The term "kinship care" covers a wide variety of arrangements under which children are cared for by family members or friends. However, the LAC Regs 2009 deal with specific kinship care arrangements for looked after children. Local authorities may formally approve kinship carers for looked after children. Unlike foster carers, kinship carers are approved to care for specific looked after children, and they may be approved only by local authorities. Kinship carers must be related to the child they are caring for or be people who are 'known to the child or with whom the child has a pre-existing relationship' (reg.10(2)).

LAC Regs 2009, particularly regs.10 to 16, reg.33 and Schedules 3 to 5

10.21

Children living with approved kinship carers are looked after in one of a variety of ways – see Chapter 9, paragraph 9.2. The arrangements for these children, as for all looked after children, are covered by the local authority duties in the LAC Regs 2009. The same regulations also cover all aspects of kinship carers' assessment, approval, etc, and placement with kinship carers.

1995 Act, s.25 and s.26; 2007 Act, s.80; 2011 Act, s.91 and 119; LAC Regs 2009, including regs.10 to 16, reg.33 and Schedules 3 to 5

10.22

For kinship carers, the LAC Regs 2009 cover:

● the assessment and approval of kinship carers;

- placements in kinship care and notifications of them;

- short-term placements – respite care;

- case records for kinship carers; and

- kinship care allowances.

There are also Schedules which set out the information to be obtained about prospective kinship carers when they are assessed; matters to be covered in individual Kinship Carer Agreements, i.e. contracts between kinship carers and the authority which approved them; and matters to be covered in individual Kinship Placement Agreements, about each child placed.

LAC Regs 2009

10.23

There is no requirement for local authorities to have kinship care panels, but some local authorities have established these. Other local authorities use their fostering or other panels to consider kinship carer approvals.

10.24

Kinship carers do not acquire parental responsibilities and rights (PRRs) simply because of the placements. Carers have general duties and rights in relation to the children in their care under s.5 of the 1995 Act, and may be able to consent to medical treatment – see Chapter 6, paragraph 6.2. Kinship carers who look after children who are subject to compulsory supervision orders (CSOs), and interim CSOs may be 'deemed' relevant persons for the purposes of the hearing system – see Chapter 11, paragraphs 11.16 to 11.18. Kinship carers who look after children under POs or POAs may have some PRRs for them, depending on the terms of the individual order – see Chapter 12, particularly paragraphs 12.5 to 12.7 and 12.31.

1995 Act, s.5; 2011 Act, s.81; 2007 Act, ss.80 and 82

2014 Act: support for kinship care

10.25

When it is in force, the 2014 Act provides for 'kinship care assistance', which is *not* for children who are looked after. The assistance is to provide support for carers who have or are applying for a 'kinship care order' for children under 16 who are at risk of becoming looked after or fit another description set out in subordinate legislation. A 'kinship care order' is defined as certain types of order granted under s.11 of the 1995 Act, giving residence or guardianship rights to the carers. In addition, carers must be relatives or friends or have another connection as set out in the subordinate legislation. Local authorities will have a duty to provide kinship care assistance to carers in their area. The assistance includes counselling, advice or information, financial support, service provisions and other help set out in the subordinate legislation. Many of the details of the support scheme are dependent on what is in the subordinate legislation.

The Children's Hearing system

This chapter provides some basic information about children's hearings and how they operate, including the involvement of the children's reporter, SCRA, Children's Hearings Scotland, local authorities and others. The 2011 Act and the CH Rules 2013 are complex and this chapter only gives a simple outline.

The system

11.1
___
The Scottish Children's Hearing system was introduced by the Social Work (Scotland) Act 1968. It was an innovation of large proportions resulting from the *Kilbrandon Report* and replacing the former juvenile court system. The system deals with children who commit crimes and all other children with social problems. Since its introduction, children charged with a crime are dealt with in the adult system only if the crime is a more serious one (see Chapter 3). Most crimes where children under 16 are charged are reported by the police to the reporter only, and not to the PF (see Chapter 3).

11.2
___
The system is not concerned with guilt or innocence but the welfare principle: what is in the child's best interests. This principle applies whether the child has offended or has been offended against. In other words, one system deals with both juvenile criminal justice and children's welfare.

11.3
___
When the system was first introduced it dealt largely with criminal cases,

but over the years, more and more cases have been concerned with child protection in its wider sense, as awareness of this has increased.

11.4

The 1995 Act repealed that part of the 1968 Act dealing with the hearing system, and re-enacted it. There were some changes to and updating of the system, taking account of the lapse of time since the 1968 Act, and also various reports, including the Clyde enquiry into the Orkney case. Nonetheless, the essence of the hearing system, as introduced in 1968, remained much the same, including the pre-eminence of the welfare principle. On 24 June 2013, the 2011 Act repealed and replaced that part of the 1995 Act dealing with the hearing system. Much of the hearing system has continued as before, albeit with new section numbers and new terminology. However, there are some important changes, and the 2011 Act is longer and more complex than the provisions in the 1995 Act. There is a lot of secondary legislation, including for secure accommodation.

11.5

Each hearing has a panel of three lay members, who make the decisions, called children's panel members. They were formerly appointed by the Scottish Ministers. The 2011 Act established Children's Hearings Scotland (CHS) as a separate, independent organisation for the management of all matters for panel members. CHS has a Board of Management and the Chief Executive is the National Convener. Since 24 June 2013, all panel members are appointed by CHS, and are members of the National Panel for Scotland. CHS manages all aspects of panel member recruitment, selection, appointment, training and practice development, monitoring, complaints and expenses.

2011 Act, ss.1 to 13 and Schedules 1, 2 and 4

11.6

When a hearing is held, it must consist of three panel members, of whom one must be a man and one a woman. One panel member with experience and appropriate training acts as the chairing member, although he or she has no overriding vote. Decisions are made unanimously or by majority.

2011 Act, ss.5 to 7

11.7

The reporter to the children's panel or children's reporter acts in some ways like a clerk to a hearing, but he or she has many other duties throughout the wider system. From 1 April 1996, the reporter's service has operated on a national basis as the Scottish Children's Reporter Administration (SCRA). From 24 June 2013, the 2011 Act provides the legislative basis for SCRA. There is a Principal Reporter and SCRA has nine localities, supported by a Head Office. The system is independent of and separate from the system whereby panel members are appointed by CHS.

2011 Act, ss.14 to 24 and Schedule 3

Referral to the reporter

11.8

Anyone *may* provide information or refer a child to the reporter where the person considers:

(a) *that the child is in need of protection, guidance, treatment or control, and*

(b) *that it might be necessary for a compulsory supervision order to be made in relation to the child.*

When the local authority considers this applies to a child, they have a *duty* to enquire into the child's circumstances and to refer to the reporter. The police also have a *duty* to refer and any other person *may* do so. The bulk of referrals come from the local authority, including social work and education departments, the police and health services.

2011 Act, ss.60 to 64

11.9

Anyone making a referral will probably think about the possible grounds of referral (see paragraph 11.14 below) but the decisions about whether there are grounds, and if so, which ones apply, are for the reporter (see below, paragraphs 11.10 to 11.13). This means that if any person or body is concerned about a child, they can refer whether or not they are certain about grounds for referral.

11.10

A child in the hearing system is usually under 16. However, once a child is subject to a CSO, he or she may stay in the system until the age of 18. Any child under 16 may be referred to the reporter; and the reporter may refer a child who is not already subject to a CSO to a hearing after the child's 16th birthday, provided that the referral was received before that date. In practice, the referral of a child to the reporter near his or her 16th birthday may be of little assistance to the child if the child is not already subject to a CSO.

2011 Act, s.199

Reporter's duties and options

11.11

When a child has been referred to the reporter, he or she must decide whether a ground for referral applies and, if so, whether a CSO is necessary for the child. The reporter has three options and must decide:

- that a hearing is not required and inform the child's family, etc, of this decision; *or*

- that a hearing is not necessary but that it is appropriate to refer the case to the local authority to provide 'advice, guidance and assistance to the child and the child's family' in terms of the local authority's duties in ss.16 to 38 of the 1995 Act; *or*

- to arrange a children's hearing because the reporter thinks that a CSO is "necessary" for the child – in other words, an order seems needed.

2011 Act, ss.66 to 69

11.12

Where a reporter has arranged a hearing, he or she must request a report on the child from the local authority, unless one has already been done as part of the initial investigation. Further additional information may be sought from the local authority.

2011 Act, s.69

11.13

In essence, the reporter's decision to proceed to a hearing is made on the basis that:

- the child needs compulsory measures of supervision, i.e. there is a basis for statutory intervention, looking at the child's welfare; *and*
- there is sufficient evidence to establish one or more of the grounds for referral in s.67 – see below.

2011 Act, s.66

Section 67 grounds, for referral to a hearing

11.14

The grounds for referring a child to a hearing are in s.67 of the 2011 Act and are called 'section 67 grounds'. These are that:

(a) the child is likely to suffer unnecessarily, or is likely to have his or her health or development seriously impaired, due to a lack of parental care;

(b) the child has had committed against him or her any of the offences listed in Schedule 1 to the Criminal Procedure (Scotland) Act 1995;

(c) the child has, or is likely to have, a close connection with a person who has committed a Schedule 1 offence;

(d) the child is, or is likely to become, a member of the same household as a child in respect of whom a Schedule 1 offence has been committed;

(e) the child is being, or is likely to be, exposed to persons whose conduct is (or has been) such that it is likely that –

   (i) the child will be abused or harmed, or

   (ii) the child's health, safety or development will be seriously adversely affected;

(f) the child has, or is likely to have, a close connection with a person who has carried out domestic abuse;

(g) the child has, or is likely to have, a close connection with a person who has committed an offence under Parts 1, 4 or 5 of the Sexual Offences (Scotland) Act 2009;

(h) the child is being provided with accommodation by a local authority under s.25 of the 1995 Act and special measures are needed to support the child;

(i) a permanence order is in force in respect of the child and special measures are needed to support the child;

(j) the child has committed an offence;

(k) the child has misused alcohol;

(l) the child has misused a drug (whether or not a controlled drug);

(m) the child's conduct has had, or is likely to have, a serious adverse effect on the health, safety or development of the child or another person;

(n) the child is beyond the control of a relevant person;

(o) the child has failed without reasonable excuse to attend regularly at school;

(p) the child –

  (i) is being, or is likely to be, subjected to physical, emotional or other pressure to enter into a civil partnership, or

  (ii) is, or is likely to become, a member of the same household as such a child;

(q) the child –

  (i) has been, is being or is likely to be forced into a marriage (as in s.1 of the Forced Marriage etc (Protection and Jurisdiction) (Scotland) Act 2011), or

  (ii) is, or is likely to become, a member of the same household as such a child.

2011 Act, s.67(2), as amended by the FM Act 2011, s.13

11.15

Where the grounds refer to a child having 'a close connection with a person', it means that 'the child is member of the same household as the person, or... has significant contact with the person.'

2011 Act, s.67(3)

Relevant persons, including 'deemed' relevant persons

11.16

In the 1995 Act, the term used for an adult with a range of rights in the hearing system was 'relevant person' (not "parent"). The same term is used in the 2011 Act, and a person who is a relevant person has much the same rights as under the 1995 Act. A relevant person has a range of rights, including the right to:

● be sent notification of each hearing;

● be sent all the papers, reports, etc;

- attend the child's hearing, and has a duty as well, unless the hearing is satisfied that it would be unreasonable for him or her to attend;

- bring a representative and a legal representative to each hearing;

- be asked if s.67 grounds are accepted or not;

- receive written notification of the decision of each hearing;

- attend any proof hearing and be represented;

- appeal against decisions; and

- ask for a review any time after three months from the previous decision.

2011 Act, s.74, s.78(1)(c), s.90, s.104, s.106, s.132, s.154, ss.158 to 160 and ss.162 and 163; CH Rules 2013

11.17

Under the 2011 Act, there are now two types of relevant persons: "automatic" ones and 'deemed' ones. They all have the same rights and duties, but the ways in which they are relevant persons is different. "Automatic" relevant persons are people who have the status automatically, because of the statutory definition. Their status remains for all hearings, and cannot be removed. Section 200 of the 2011 Act, as amended, says that the following people are relevant persons, "automatically":

1. a parent or guardian *with* parental responsibilities and/or rights under Part I of the 1995 Act, i.e. under Scots Law;

2. a parent *with no* parental responsibilities or rights (as long as s/he did not have them previously and then lost them through a court order);

3. a person *with* parental responsibilities and/or rights from an order made under the 1995 Act, s.11, and which gave some or all of these and/or residence, *but excluding* someone who only has a contact or specific issue order;

4. a parent *with* parental responsibility under the Children Act 1989 or Adoption and Children Act 2002, i.e. under English and Welsh law;

5. a person *with* parental responsibilities under the Children (Northern Ireland) Order 1995, i.e. under Northern Irish law; and

6. a person with parental responsibilities and/or rights under a permanence order.

This is a very different definition from the previous one in the 1995 Act. It includes all parents, whether they have all, any or no PRRs. And it excludes people ordinarily caring for children, such as grandparents and other kinship carers, and foster carers and adopters, unless they have some PRRs.

2011 Act, s.200, as added to by the Children's Hearings (Scotland) Act 2011 (Review of Contact Directions and Definition of Relevant Person) Order 2013, SSI 2013/193, paragraph 3

11.18

Other people may be deemed relevant persons by children's hearings. The child, existing relevant persons and people who wish to be relevant persons may all ask for a hearing to have someone or themselves deemed as relevant persons. The reporter may also ask for this. The hearing makes a decision at a pre-hearing panel (see paragraph 11.19) or at a full hearing. Panel members must deem someone a relevant person if they think 'that the individual has (or has recently had) a significant involvement in the upbringing of the child.' Once someone is deemed a relevant person, he or she retains that status, unless and until a future review hearing considers that he or she 'may no longer have (nor recently have had) a significant involvement in the upbringing of the child.' There are rights of appeal against a decision that someone is or is not a relevant person. Such an appeal must be made within seven days and then heard within three days.

2011 Act, ss.79 to 81, s.142, and ss.160 and 164

Hearings, pre-hearings and emergency hearings

11.19

Hearings may be held for a whole range of reasons, and may make final decisions or short-term ones. The 2011 Act introduced pre-hearing panels as well. These may deal with whether someone should or should not be deemed a relevant person, whether a child or relevant person may be excused from attending a hearing, whether the full hearing is likely to consider making a secure accommodation authorisation, and other matters in the CH Rules 2013, including about non-disclosure of information to any of the parties. When a full hearing is arranged, this could be for a range of matters, including:

- for new s.67 grounds for referral; *or*
- a continuation of an existing case; *or*
- to deal with s.67 grounds established at court; *or*
- to review an existing CSO; *or*
- to deal with a child protection emergency; *or*
- to provide advice to a criminal court or about permanence plans.

The 2011 Act and the CH Rules 2013 have detailed rules about the preparation for and the running and chairing of hearings and pre-hearing panels.

2011 Act, including ss.79 to 81; CH Rules 2013

11.20

For a full hearing, unless it is an emergency one, a reporter must usually give seven days' notice of the date, time, place, etc, to the child and relevant persons. Where grounds for referral are put, at least seven days' notice of the actual grounds themselves must be given, unless it is an eighth working day hearing after a CPO. For a pre-hearing panel, five days' notice should be given if practicable.

CH Rules 2011, including rr.22 and 23, r.27, r.29 and rr.45 and 46

11.21

A child has a right and a duty to attend his or her hearing. A child may be excused from attending if the grounds relate to offences against the child or other children and the child's attendance is not necessary for a fair hearing; *or* if attendance would put 'the child's physical, mental or moral welfare at risk'; *or* if the child 'would not be capable of understanding what happens at the hearing', taking account of age and maturity. A child can insist on attending even if excused. The child also has a right to bring a representative to the hearing and to have legal representation if he or she understands generally what it means to instruct a solicitor.

2011 Act, s.73 and s.78(1)(a) and (b); CH Rules 2013, r.11; 1991 Act, s.2(4A)

11.22

Panel members may exclude a relevant person and/or representative for any part of the hearing. They can do this if they feel it is necessary to do so in order to find out the views of the child, or if the presence of the person is causing or is likely to cause 'significant distress' to the child. Where someone is excluded in this way, the chair of the hearing must explain 'what has taken place' to him or her.

2011 Act, ss.76 and 77

11.23

Before the hearing, the child and every relevant person should be sent all the information and reports prepared for the hearing. These are the same reports which are sent to panel members, and also to any safeguarder who has been appointed. In practice, reports, etc, are not usually sent to children under 12.

CH Rules 2013, including r.18

11.24

The CH Rules 2013 contain detailed provisions about procedures for many different types of hearings. These are generally similar but vary depending on the purpose and/or outcome of each individual hearing. As indicated, at the hearing the child and any relevant person may each be accompanied by a representative. The chair must explain the purpose of the hearing and go over any s.67 grounds. He or she must explain the substance of the reports which the panel members, the relevant person(s) and the child have received. After considering the case, the panel members must reach a decision. Before the close of the hearing, the chair must tell the child and relevant person(s):

- what the decision is;

- the reasons for it; and

- any rights of appeal against the decision.

There are also rules about written notification of the decision. The decision could be to continue the hearing.

CH Rules 2013, including rr.6 and 7, r.13, rr.48 and 49, r.58 to 83, rr.86 and 87 and r.95

11.25

Generally, hearings, emergency hearings, pre-hearing panels and related court proceedings are conducted in terms of the principles of the 2011 Act – see Chapter 2, paragraphs 2.4 to 2.7. This means that panel members and courts (except in evidential hearings – see paragraph 11.29) must:

- make the welfare of the child their paramount consideration in their decisions;

- seek out and take account of the views of the child; and

- not make an order unless they think it is better to make one than not to do so.

In addition, at every hearing, the chair must ask the child if the reports 'accurately reflect any views expressed by the child'. This is not required if the chair thinks it would be inappropriate, taking account of the child's age and maturity.

2011 Act, ss.25 to 29 and s.121

11.26

Sometimes, a hearing is held in an emergency situation. For example, the child may be the subject of a CPO (see Chapter 8, including paragraph 8.14), in which case there are strict and complicated timetables within which the reporter (if he or she thinks a hearing is necessary) must bring the case to the hearing, and the panel members look at the situation. When a hearing meets on an emergency basis, it is not usually able to make a final decision. It is, however, allowed to issue an interim CSO (or interim variation of an existing CSO) for the child – see paragraph 11.32. An interim CSO after a CPO will usually be for the child to be kept in a place of safety for short periods of time, until final arrangements can be made, further investigation can be carried out and/or matters can be taken to court. But an interim CSO may have other measures as well or instead, depending on the circumstances of a case – see paragraphs 11.31 and 11.32.

2011 Act, ss.45 to 47, s.69, s.86, ss.92 to 94, ss.96 to 100, s.109, s.120

Section 67 grounds and court applications

11.27

Where a hearing has been arranged to put s.67 grounds, the Chair must explain the grounds to the child and the relevant person(s). In order to proceed any further, the panel members must be satisfied that the child and relevant person(s):

- understand the grounds; *and*

- accept them wholly or in part.

2011 Act, s.90

11.28

If the grounds for referral are fully understood and accepted by the child and relevant person(s), the hearing may go ahead. If the grounds are understood and accepted in part, the panel members may discharge the parts which are not accepted and proceed on the basis of what has been accepted. If the child and/or the relevant person(s) understand but do not accept the grounds for referral at all, or not enough to allow the hearing to proceed with an accepted part, the panel members must *either*:

- direct the reporter to make an application to the sheriff; *or*
- discharge the whole referral.

If the child is incapable of understanding or does not understand the grounds for referral, again, the hearing must either direct the reporter to apply to the sheriff or discharge the grounds, even if the relevant person(s) has/have accepted them in full.

2011 Act, s.91 to 94 and s.96

11.29

If the grounds for referral are sent to the sheriff, he or she hears evidence on the disputed facts and makes a decision based on the normal rules of evidence. If the grounds are accepted between the referral and the proof hearing, the sheriff may send them back to the hearing without a proof. If the proof goes ahead, the sheriff *either*:

- finds the s.67 grounds established in full or in part, and refers them back to a hearing; *or*
- finds them not established and discharges the whole case.

The reporter conducts the proof in front of the sheriff and the burden or onus of proof is on the reporter. All grounds must be established on the "balance of probabilities" (civil standard) except where the referred child is alleged to have committed a crime, when the standard of proof is "beyond reasonable doubt" (criminal standard). The sheriff's decision is not governed by the welfare principle because it is a straight testing of the factual evidence. The sheriff has no power to make any order about the welfare of the child in relation to the grounds, although he or she may make an interim CSO (see paragraph 11.32) if the child's welfare requires some short-term measure.

2011 Act, ss.100 to 109

Disposals by hearings: CSOs and interim CSOs

11.30

When there are accepted or established grounds, and/or there is a review of an existing CSO, a hearing has a range of options. These are:

- to discharge grounds on the basis that a CSO is not necessary;

- to continue the hearing for further information and/or investigation;

- to make a CSO or continue or vary an existing one;

- to terminate an existing CSO if it is no longer necessary, even if there are new grounds for referral.

If a case is continued and the hearing members feel that some form of compulsory measure is needed in the short term, they may make an interim CSO (see paragraph 11.32) if one has not already been made, or continue an existing one. If the hearing is reviewing a CSO, it may be continued or varied on an interim basis until the next hearing.

2007 Act, s. 91, s.97, ss.119 and 120, ss.138 to 140

11.31

A CSO is defined in s.83 of the 2011 Act. It names the 'implementation authority', the local authority responsible 'for giving effect' to the CSO; it gives the length of time the CSO will last; and it may contain one or more of the 'measures' listed in s.83(2). These are:

(a) for the child to reside at a specified place;

(b) a direction authorising restriction of the child's liberty;

(c) a prohibition on the disclosure of the child's place of residence;

(d) a movement restriction condition – see paragraph 11.51;

(e) a secure accommodation authorisation;

(f) a requirement for a specified medical or other examination or specified medical or other treatment for the child;

(g) a direction about contact between the child and others;

(h) some other specified condition on the child;

(i) some other specified duties on the implementation authority in relation to the child.

An interim CSO (see paragraph 11.32) may contain the same range of measures. And it may instead of specifying a particular place of residence, merely state that the child is to reside 'at any place of safety'. Children may be looked after in many different ways on CSOs and interim CSOs, including at home, in foster care, in kinship care, with prospective adopters, in residential placements and in secure accommodation.

2007 Act, s.83 to 87, especially s.83(1) and (2) and s.86(1) and (2)

11.32

An interim CSO is defined in s.86 of the 2011 Act. It names the 'implementation authority' – the local authority responsible 'for giving effect' to the interim CSO; it gives the length of time the CSO will last; and it may contain one or more of the 'measures' listed for CSOs in s.83(2) – see paragraph 11.31. This order was introduced by the 2011 Act and replaces a warrant to keep a child in a place of safety and also provides many other short-term options. An interim CSO may be issued by hearings or sheriffs, and can last for up to 22 days. It may be renewed by hearings on some occasions and by sheriffs. If there is an existing CSO for a child, the order is called an interim variation of that CSO. There is a right of appeal against any interim CSO, and when an appeal is lodged, it must be heard within three days.

2007 Act, s.83 to 87, s.96, ss.98 to 100, s.109, s.120, ss.154 to 157

11.33

Local authorities must carry out the terms of CSOs. This includes making sure that: children are living where their CSOs require; other conditions are being carried out; and they are implementing any duties specifically imposed on them in CSOs – see paragraph 11.31(i). If hearings feel that local authorities are not complying with their duty, they may authorise the National Convener (see paragraph 11.5) to apply to the Sheriff Principal about the breach. The Sheriff Principal may make orders requiring the local authorities to perform the duties. These provisions about enforcement of local authority duties replace earlier ones in the ASBA 2004 – see paragraph 11.46.

2011 Act, ss.144 to 148

Reviews

11.34

It is and always has been an essential part of the hearing system that no order may last for more than one year without being reviewed. If a supervision requirement is not reviewed within a year, it automatically falls.

2011 Act, s.83(7)

11.35

The 2011 Act contains a wide range of possible reviews, including some new ones. Children, relevant persons, the local authority, and hearing members may request reviews, and the reporter has duties to arrange others. The main reviews are where:

- the local authority consider a review is necessary;

- the local authority are planning permanent arrangements for the child (PO, POA or adoption) or an adoption application is proposed;

- the child wishes a review (provided the CSO was made, continued or varied more than three months before);

- a relevant person wishes a review (provided the CSO was made or varied more than three months before);

- hearing members wish the CSO reviewed; and

- the CSO will expire in less than three months, in which case the reporter arranges an "annual review".

There are also reviews of secure accommodation authorisations, emergency transfers, movement restriction conditions and of contact directions. If there is a full review hearing, it may also consider whether a deemed relevant person should continue to be deemed.

2011 Act, s.125 and 126, ss.129 to 136, ss.142 and 143

11.36

There is also an automatic review when the reporter puts new grounds for referral to a child who is already subject to a CSO.

2011 Act, s.97, and s.91 as modified by s.97

11.37

The need for there to be a review when the local authority are planning for permanence means that hearing members must discuss plans for long-term care and adoption and give their opinion on them.

2011 Act, s.131(2)(c) to (e) and s.141

Appeals

11.38

There are rights of appeal within the hearing system. An appeal may be made against: a final decision about a CSO; or a decision about an interim CSO (see paragraph 11.32); or a decision about a medical examination order; or the granting of a warrant to secure the child's attendance at a hearing. An appeal must usually be made within three weeks of the decision, to the sheriff. Certain appeals must be heard and disposed of within three days. These are where the appeal is against the making of: a CSO with a secure accommodation authorisation, an interim CSO, an interim variation of a CSO, a medical examination order or a warrant to secure the child's attendance.

2011 Act, ss.154 to 157

11.39

When a sheriff is dealing with an appeal against an interim CSO, or a medical examination order or a warrant, he or she must either uphold the decision or terminate or recall the order. When a sheriff is dealing with a decision about a CSO, he or she has a range of options. He or she may confirm the decision with or without further steps; or continue or vary the order appealed against; or overturn the decision, terminate any order and discharge the child from any further proceedings; or may order that a new children's hearing is arranged; or make an interim CSO or interim variation of an existing CSO; or grant a warrant to secure attendance.

2011 Act, s.156

11.40

There are further rights of appeal from the sheriff to the Sheriff Principal or straight to the Court of Session. This can be against *either* a sheriff's appeal decision *or* against a sheriff's finding that grounds for referral are established or not established. The reporter has a right to appeal in most situations at this stage, as well as the child, relevant person(s) and the safeguarder. If an appeal is made to the Sheriff Principal, it is possible to appeal again to the Court of Session, with the leave of the Sheriff Principal.

2011 Act, s.163

11.41

There are other appeal provisions in the 2011 Act. Appeals may be made to the sheriff against decisions about: whether someone should or should not be deemed a relevant person; contact rights for someone who is not a relevant person (see paragraph 11.18); and implementation or not of a secure accommodation authorisation. Further appeals may be made to the Sheriff Principal and/or the Court of Session. There is also a right to review when a local authority wish to challenge the fact that they have been named as the implementation authority in a CSO, interim CSO or medical examination order. After the sheriff has reviewed the matter, there may be an appeal to the Sheriff Principal, whose decision is final.

2011 Act, ss.160 to 162 and ss.164 to 167

Safeguarders

11.42

Safeguarders were introduced into the Children's Hearing system in 1985 and have continued under the 1995 and 2011 Acts. A safeguarder may be appointed by a children's hearing in any case, or by a sheriff who is dealing grounds for referral, appeals or reviews of grounds established. A pre-hearing panel may also appoint one.

2011 Act, ss.30 and 31 and s.82

11.43

The function of a safeguarder is essentially to provide an "independent" view of the child's case. He or she should look at the case from the perspective of the child's best interests. A safeguarder will usually provide a report for the hearing or court, setting out what he or she thinks is relevant to the child's case, from the perspective mentioned.

11.44

A safeguarder has the right to attend hearings, and should do so. He or she must be notified of hearings in the same way as the child and relevant persons; and should also be provided with reports, etc, and sent reasons for hearing decisions. A safeguarder may appeal against definitive hearing decisions, and against certain decisions of the sheriff. A safeguarder's appointment ceases (terminates) at the end of the time allowed for an appeal (21 days) after the hearing has made, varied, or terminated a CSO for the child, or discharged the case. However, if there is an appeal, the appointment continues until the appeal processes have been completed.

CH Rules 2013, rr.22 and 26 and r.88; 2011 Act s.154, s.163 and s.34

11.45

There are regulations with detailed provisions about safeguarders. There is a national Safeguarders Panel for Scotland, and its management and operation is carried out by Children 1st. There is some information on their website – see Further Reading.

Antisocial Behaviour etc (Scotland) Act 2004 and related matters

11.46

This Act introduced a number of provisions which affected children and young people and which could involve the reporter, hearings and/or the courts. The provisions were not really part of the hearing system, but it is convenient to mention them here, particularly as some have now been moved into the 2011 Act. The matters still in the 2004 Act include allowing sheriffs to make antisocial behaviour orders (ASBOs) in relation to young people over 12 with or without referring the child to the reporter; allowing courts to make parenting orders; and allowing courts to "tag" young people under 16. The 2011 Act now provides for other matters introduced by the 2004 Act. Hearings may make movement restriction conditions in CSOs and interim CSO; hearings may impose specific duties on local authorities in CSOs and interim CSOs; and Sheriffs Principal may order local authorities to perform duties when they are in breach of them.

11.47

Local authorities may apply to the sheriff for ASBOs for anyone who is 12 or over. If the person for whom the ASBO is sought is under 16, the sheriff must ask for a hearing to give advice, to see if the ASBO "is necessary". It is an offence to breach an ASBO, but no one under 16 can be imprisoned for that. When an ASBO is made for someone under 16, the sheriff may also ask the reporter to fix a hearing. If the young person is not already subject to CSO, the hearing will be on the basis of whichever s.67 grounds the sheriff considers appropriate, but these cannot be that the child has committed an offence. The s.67 grounds are already established by virtue of the referral from the sheriff. If the young person is already subject to a CSO, the reporter must fix a review hearing.

ASBA 2004, s.4, ss.9 and 10 and s.12 as amended by the 2011 Act; 2011 Act, s.70 and s.129

11.48

A parenting order under the ASBA 2004 requires a person to comply with the requirements in it and to attend counselling or guidance sessions. When a court is considering parental orders, the child's welfare is the paramount consideration.

ASBA s.103 and s.109

11.49

A sheriff may make a parenting order when he or she makes an ASBO in respect of someone under 16. This can be done if the sheriff thinks an 'order is desirable in the interest of preventing the child from engaging in further antisocial behaviour'. There also have to be local arrangements for parental order compliance.

ASBA 2004, s.13

11.50

Parenting orders may also be made on the application of a local authority or the reporter, if there are local arrangements. Courts and hearings can direct the reporter to consider applying for an order. The court has to be satisfied about certain conditions before granting orders. There are provisions about reviews, variations and failures to comply.

ASBA 2004, s.102, s.114, s.105, s.107 and s.109; 2011 Act, s.128 (replacing 1995 Act, s.75A, which was inserted by 2004 Act, s.116)

11.51

Courts can make restriction of liberty orders – "tagging" – for young people under 16. Hearings may make CSOs and interim CSOs with movement restriction conditions – see paragraph 11.31.

ASBA 2004, s.121; 2011 Act, ss.83, 84 and 86.

Permanence orders (POs and POAs)

This chapter deals with permanence orders (POs), and permanence orders with authority for adoption (POAs).

Introduction

12.1

POs and POAs are orders which are designed as an option for children who are not able to live at home. They give local authorities some or possibly all parental responsibilities and rights (PRRs). They may also give some PRRs to carers such as foster or kinship carers; and they take some or possibly all PRRs away from parents. They were introduced by the 2007 Act and the background and theory are set out in Chapter 5 of the 2005 APRG Phase II Report. They are designed to be as flexible as possible, different for each child, to meet his or her individual needs. All children who are the subject of POs or POAs are looked after by the local authority; and all orders last until the child is 18, unless they are revoked or the child is adopted.

APRG Report, 2005, Chapter 5; 2007 Act, particularly ss.80 to 104; 1995 Act, s.17(6) as amended

12.2

A permanence order may be a "destination" one (usually a PO) *or* the route to adoption (usually but not always a POA). However, if adoption is the plan for a child, it is not essential to seek a POA first. Only a local authority may apply for a PO or POA, although parents and others have rights to be parties to all court proceedings. Every order gives the local authority at least one parental responsibility and one right, and may give them other PRRs. However, the flexibility arises from the fact that the parents may keep some PRRs, as appropriate in each case, and/or other people, such as foster or kinship carers, may be given some PRRs, again as appropriate in each case.

12.3

A PO may have up to three parts:

1. the mandatory provision, the essential part of the order;

2. ancillary provisions, not essential but every order should have some; and

3. authority for adoption, but only if adoption is the plan for the child.

2007 Act, ss.80 to 82

Mandatory provision

12.4

Every PO and POA has the mandatory provision and there cannot be an order unless this is part of it. The mandatory provision is given to the local authority which applied for the order and is the heart or kernel of a PO. It has two parts: the parental responsibility to provide the child with guidance; and the parental right to regulate the child's residence, that is, where the child lives. Also, as an automatic part of the order, the parents'/guardians' parental right to control residence is removed.

2007 Act, ss.80, 81 and 87, with reference to 1995 Act, ss.1 and 2

Ancillary provisions

12.5

If a PO is granted with just the mandatory provision, no other PRRs are automatically given to the local authority or removed from the parents. If the applicant local authority wants more PRRs, and wants foster or kinship carers to acquire PRRs, and/or wants some or all of the parents' other PRRs to be removed, they need to ask the court to do this specifically, as part of the ancillary provisions. It is not essential for a PO to have any ancillary provisions. However, if there are no ancillary provisions, it will be difficult to make the PO work well for the benefit of the child; and it will not be possible to vary the order in the future.

2007 Act, s.80, s.82 and s.92

12.6

Ancillary provisions are about PRRs and other matters to do with the child's welfare. They are the key to an order and what gives it the flexibility needed to suit each child and his or her circumstances. It is the court which decides what provisions to give and to whom, and what PRRs to take away and from whom. This is done by including ancillary provisions in the order. The local authority applying for an order should plan for and seek the best, most flexible combination of responsibilities, rights, etc, for each child. There should be careful assessment and planning, involving social work and legal practitioners, and others as well.

2007 Act, ss.80 and 82

12.7

There are a wide range of possible ancillary provisions and a wide range of options for the court. The court may:

- give one or more parental responsibilities and/or rights to the local authority; and/or

- give one or more parental responsibilities and/or rights to other people; and/or

- take away one or more parental responsibilities and/or rights from the parents; and/or

- provide for contact arrangements for the child, and not just with the parents; and/or

- provide for any other orders about PRRs and anything else affecting the child's welfare.

Authority for adoption

12.8

This is the third possible part of a PO, and if it is granted, the order is referred to as a permanence order with authority for adoption – a POA. Unlike mandatory and ancillary provisions, many POs do not have this authority, as it is not appropriate unless adoption is the plan for the child. When authority for adoption is granted, it means that the court has dealt with parental consent to adoption: the consent has either been given or dispensed with by the court on one of the statutory grounds. As a result, consent to adoption should not be an issue in the subsequent adoption, and, to that extent, authority for adoption is similar to freeing. However, the overall effect of the POA is not as rigid as freeing was. For instance, there may be an ancillary provision giving contact, direct or indirect, to the parents. And unlike a freeing order, a POA makes a child looked after until the adoption is granted and the whole order ceases to have effect, or the order is otherwise revoked.

2007 Act, s.80, s.83, s.102 and s.100

Pre-court procedures

12.9

The decision to apply for a PO or POA is taken by the local authority's "agency decision maker" after their own internal reviews and administrative procedures. There are considerations or principles which apply to local authority planning for any PO or POA application – see Chapter 2. Local authority duties are in s.17 of the 1995 Act and the LAC Regs 2009, because planning for a PO or POA will almost always be work carried out for a looked after child, and any child subject to a PO or POA is looked after.

1995 Act, s.17; LAC Regs 2009; and possibly Ad Ag Regs 2009

12.10

When a PO is the plan for a child, the Ad Ag Regs 2009 do not apply to the local authority processes. This means that there is no duty on a local authority to take their plans for a PO to their adoption/permanence panel, although many local authorities choose to do this. Also, there are no timescales for any of the period between making the looked after review decision to seek permanence away from home and lodging the court application. When a PO is the plan, whether the case is considered by the panel or not, the authority make a formal decision to apply to the court. This decision should be intimated to the parents and others as appropriate, including the child when he or she is older.

12.11

When a POA is the plan for a child, the local authority must follow the processes set out in the Ad Ag Regs 2009 before applying to the court, because the overall plan is for adoption. The processes required for adoption applications are covered in Chapter 13, paragraphs 13.19 to 13.21. They are similar to and overlap with those outlined in paragraphs 12.12 to 12.14 below. Sometimes, a child may already be placed for adoption, but the local authority wish to proceed with a POA anyway, before the adoption application. However, a POA is not mandatory for an agency adoption to go ahead.

Ad Ag Regs 2009

12.12

As in a direct agency adoption application, there are complicated regulations about procedures and timescales before a POA may be applied for. The local authority must refer their plan for a POA to their adoption/permanence panel, for a recommendation about whether adoption is in the child's best interests with a POA, and registration of the child for adoption. There are then timescales from the panel recommendations being made through to notifications to parents and beyond, if the plan is opposed. If the birth parents indicate within a certain time that they are in agreement with the plan for adoption with a POA, the agency can go ahead without further timescales. If, however, the parents refuse to agree, or do not return the notifications within a set time, the local authority is tied by strict timescales. It must apply for a POA or ensure that an adoption application is lodged by adoptive parents within very short timescales.

Ad Ag Regs 2009, reg.6, regs.12 to 17 and regs.20 to 23; also reg.18 and reg.23A

12.13

When a child is subject to a CSO and permanence plans are made, there are additional requirements. The plan may be for a PO on its own, or for adoption with or without a POA. The child must be referred to a hearing for it to review the CSO and provide written "advice" to the court about the plans. If adoption is planned, with or without a POA, and the parents and/or the hearing do not agree with the plans, there are further detailed timescales.

2011 Act, s.131, ss.137 and 138 and s.141; Ad Ag Regs 2009, regs.22 and 23

12.14

In every PO and POA application, the local authority must prepare and lodge a detailed report for the court with the application or petition. There are detailed court rules about what the report should cover.

Sheriff Court Adoption Rules 2009, r.31(2)(b) and (3); RCS r.67.28(2)(b) and (3)

Court procedures for POs and POAs

12.15

POs and POAs may be applied for in the sheriff court or the Court of Session. In every application, whether agreed or not, the court has to be satisfied about a number of conditions and considerations, including the principles set out in Chapter 2 – see paragraph 12.22. Court procedures for all POs and POAs are very similar to those for adoption applications – see Chapter 13, paragraphs 13.22 to 13.33. Where the child resides in Scotland at the time an application is made for a PO or POA, it may be heard in the Court of Session or in the local sheriff court. The decision about where to apply is made by the authority making the application. Most cases are dealt with in the sheriff court. If the child resides outwith Scotland at the time the application is made, the application must be made in the Court of Session and may only be for a POA. It is not possible to apply for a PO when the child does not live in Scotland.

2007 Act, ss.83 and 84, s.14 and s.118

12.16

Forms are provided with the court rules for PO and POA applications or petitions. These are in appendices to the rules, but the easiest way to obtain up-to-date versions is from the courts directly, or from the Scottish Courts website – see Further Reading. Forms are completed and lodged in court, along with other documents such as the child's birth certificate and the detailed local authority report.

Sheriff Court Adoption Rules 2009, r.31, especially r.31(2); RCS r.67.28, especially r.67.28(2)

12.17

Once the PO or POA petition is lodged, court rules have timetables for dealing with the different stages of the application, particularly in disputed cases. The court arranges a preliminary hearing to take place within eight weeks, and will appoint a curator, and in POA applications, also appoint a reporting officer. The applicant has to intimate the application and the hearing date to the birth parents and anyone else the court thinks should receive notice. Anyone who wishes to oppose the application must lodge a form of response saying this, within 21 days.

Sheriff Court Adoption Rules 2009, rr.32 to 38; RCS rr.67.29 to 67.32

12.18

The curator is an independent person providing a view of the case from the perspective of the child's welfare. He or she must also give the child's views to the court, provided the child wishes to give them to the curator. The curator is often the same person as the reporting officer, but not always. The curator should report back to the court within four weeks.

Sheriff Court Adoption Rules 2009, rr.32 and 44; RCS rr.67.29 and 67.38

12.19

A reporting officer is appointed in all POA cases but in PO applications only when the child is 12 or over. He or she is concerned with the consent or non-consent to the application. If a POA is being sought, the reporting officer has to find out if the parents agree to adoption. When the application is for a PO or POA and the child is aged 12 or over, the reporting officer also has to find out whether the child consents or not. When parents and/or the child agree with the application, the reporting officer obtains their formal written consents. If the parents and/or the child do not agree, he or she reports this to the court. The reporting officer should report back to the court within four weeks.

Sheriff Court Adoption Rules 2009, r.32 and r.44; RCS r.67.29 and r.67.38

12.20

At the preliminary hearing, if there is no opposition to the application, the court may grant the order or continue the matter for further information, etc. Even when the birth parents have consented, the court must be satisfied about the principles in the 2007 Act – see Chapter 2 and paragraph 12.22. If there is no opposition in a POA application, but the birth parents have not formally consented, the court will have to be satisfied that their consent may be dispensed with, although there may not be a full evidential proof – see paragraphs 12.23 and 12.24.

2007 Act, s.84, s.14 and s.83; Sheriff Court Adoption Rules 2009, r.35; RCS, r.67.31

12.21

If the birth parents are opposing the application, the local authority must lodge a brief statement of the facts they will be relying on, and this must then be answered by or on behalf of the birth parents. A proof hearing will be fixed, which should be within 16 weeks, and a pre-proof hearing is also arranged in most cases, to enable the court to find out if the parties are properly prepared. In the sheriff court, Practice Notes for each Sheriffdom give further directions about procedures to be followed – see Further Reading.

Sheriff Court Adoption Rules 2009, rr.34A to 37; RCS rr.67.31 and 67.32

12.22

In every application for a PO or POA, the court must take account of a range of principles, conditions and considerations. It must make its decision on the basis of the principles in the 2007 Act – see Chapter 2. When the child is 12 or over, the court must also be satisfied that he or she consents to the PO or POA. As well as the principles, in every PO and POA application, the court must also be satisfied that one of the "grounds" is established. These are *either* that there is no one who has the parental right to control the child's residence, that is the right to say where the child should live; *or*, if there is someone who has this right, that it would be 'seriously detrimental to the welfare of the child' for him or her to live with the person, that is, it would be 'seriously detrimental' for the child to live at home. The first ground will be satisfied if there is no parent with the right to control residence. However, in many cases, there will be at least one parent who has that right, so the local authority have to show that it would be 'seriously detrimental' for the child to return to live with the parent(s).

2007 Act, s.84, including s.84(5)(c), and s.14 for POA applications

12.23

When the application is for a POA, there are four additional tests which have to be met before a court may grant the order. These are in addition to those mentioned in paragraph 12.22 and Chapter 2. These additional matters are that:

- the local authority have asked for authority for adoption in their application;

- the court is satisfied that the child has been placed for adoption or is likely to be placed for adoption;

- the court is satisfied that either the parents consent to adoption or the consent should be dispensed with – see paragraph 12.24; and

- the court thinks that it would be better for the child that it grants the authority for adoption rather than not grant it the "minimum necessary intervention" test.

2007 Act, s.83(1), with s.83(2) to (5)

12.24

If the parents do not consent to the POA and adoption, there are five grounds for dispensing with parental consent. They are the same as those used in adoption applications – see Chapter 13, paragraph 13.30. The grounds are that:

1. the parent or guardian is dead, s.83(2)(a);

2. the parent or guardian cannot be found or is incapable of consenting, s.83(2)(b);

3. the parent or guardian –

   - has parental responsibilities or rights *and*

   - cannot, in the court's opinion, 'satisfactorily...discharge' those parental responsibilities or exercise those parental rights *and*

   - 'is likely to continue to be unable to do so', s.83(3);

4. the parent or guardian -

   - has lost all parental responsibilities or rights through a permanence order which does not give authority for adoption, (i.e. a PO not a POA) *and*

   - is 'unlikely' to be given back such responsibilities or rights, s.83(4).

5. Where neither of the previous two grounds (i.e. 3 and 4) apply, the child's welfare 'otherwise requires the consent to be dispensed with', s.83(2)(d).

2007 Act, s.83(1)(c), (2), (3), (4) and (5)

12.25

In a disputed PO, when the birth parents are opposing the application, the court considers all the evidence about the case. If the court is satisfied evidentially, it still has to decide whether to grant the PO, on the basis of the welfare and other principles (see Chapter 2).

12.26

In a disputed POA, when the birth parents are opposing the application, the local authority have to ask the court to dispense with their consent on one of the grounds listed in s.83(2) to (4) of the 2007 Act. The court considers all the evidence in order to decide whether to dispense with consent on one of the grounds listed in paragraph 12.24. If the court is satisfied evidentially, it still has to decide whether to dispense with the consent, and then whether to grant the POA, on the basis of the welfare and other principles (see Chapter 2).

12.27

When a court grants a PO or POA and the child is subject to a compulsory supervision order, the court must revoke the CSO unless it thinks the child still needs compulsory measures under the Children's Hearing system.

2007 Act, s.89

12.28

When a court grants a PO or a POA or refuses to grant an order, there is a right of appeal. If the application was made in the sheriff court, an appeal may be made to the Sheriff Principal and/or to the Inner House of the Court of Session. If the application was made in the Court of Session, an appeal may be made to the Inner House of the Court of Session. A further appeal is possible to the Supreme Court.

Children's hearings and permanence orders

12.29

If there is a pending court application for a PO, POA, amendment or variation, there are restrictions on the decisions which children's hearings may make about the child. If a hearing wants to vary an existing CSO for the child or make a new CSO, it cannot do so unless the court agrees. The hearing makes its decision and must then prepare a report for the court about its intentions. There are regulations about the contents of the report and rules about the court process. The provisions are complex and cause difficulties, especially when the child has been matched for an adoption placement.

2007 Act, ss.95 and 96; Adoption and Children (Scotland) Act 2007 (Supervision Requirement Reports in Applications for Permanence Orders) Regulations 2009, SSI 2009/169; Sheriff Court Adoption Rules 2009, r.51; RCS rr.67.43

12.30

When there is a PO or POA for a child, and the child is also the subject of a CSO, the local authority must not act incompatibly with the CSO.

2007 Act, s.90

Effects of POs and POAs

12.31

The effect of each PO or POA depends on the particular terms of the order, but every child subject to a PO or POA is looked after by the local authority – see Chapter 9. Every order gives the local authority the mandatory provision – see paragraph 12.4 – so the local authority controls where the child lives. The effect of a PO with ancillary provision otherwise depends on what is in the order, how many other rights and responsibilities have been given to the local authority and/or others such as carers, and how many have been taken away from the parents. The effect of a POA also partly depends on what the ancillary provisions are. But every POA has authority for adoption, so the birth parents' consent to adoption has been dealt with and should not be an issue in the subsequent adoption.

1995 Act, s.17(6) as amended; 2007 Act, ss.80 to 82 and ss.87 and 88

12.32

When there is a PO or a POA for a child, there are restrictions on the use of s.11 of the 1995 Act. A court may not make an order under s.11, unless the application is for an interdict, appointment of a judicial factor for the child or appointment or removal of someone as the child's guardian. This is because the PO or POA sets out who has what PRRs, and any changes should be applied for in a variation or revocation of that order.

1995 Act, s.11A inserted by the 2007 Act, s.103

Variation, amendment and revocation of POs and POAs

12.33

A PO or POA may have its ancillary provisions varied, or it may be revoked. A PO may be amended to have authority for adoption added. When there is any application for variation, amendment or revocation of a PO or POA, the court must apply three of the general principles referred to in Chapter 2. It must:

- treat the child's welfare through childhood (or life if an amendment is sought) as its paramount consideration;

- seek and take account of the child's views, bearing in mind the child's age and maturity; and

- have regard to the child's religious persuasion, racial, cultural and linguistic heritage.

2007 Act, s.92, s.93 and s.98, referring back to s.84(4), (5)(a) and (b) and (6)

12.34

Local authorities which hold a PO or POA must apply to court for variation of the ancillary provisions or for revocation of the order in certain circumstances. These are if there has been a 'material change' in relation to matters covered in the order, provided they think that the change means the order should be varied or revoked.

2007 Act, s.99

12.35

Anyone with an interest, including the child, the birth parents and the local authority, may apply to the sheriff for variation of the ancillary provisions of a PO or a POA. However, everyone, except the local authority, must have the leave of the court to go ahead with a full application. Leave must be granted if the court is satisfied 'that there has been a material change of circumstance' or if there is another reason to allow the application to go ahead. When deciding whether to grant leave, the court has to take account of the child's welfare and the circumstances of the birth parents, anyone with some PRRs and others. If there are no ancillary provisions in the original order, no variation is possible.

2007 Act, s.92, s.94(4) to (6)

12.36

Local authorities which hold a PO may apply to amend the order by having authority for adoption added. In other words, they may ask the court to make it a POA. The court must be satisfied about three of the four matters listed in paragraph 12.23. These are that the child has been placed for adoption or is likely to be placed for adoption; the parents consent to an adoption or the consent should be dispensed with; and it would be better for the child that there is authority for adoption rather than not. If parental consent to adoption is not given, the court may dispense with it on the basis of the same grounds as in a POA or adoption application – see paragraph 12.24. If the amendment is granted, the PO becomes a POA.

2007 Act, 93(2) to (4) referring back to s.83

12.37

The local authority or any other person affected by the order may apply to the sheriff for revocation of a PO or POA. However, everyone, except the local authority, must have the leave of the court to go ahead with a full application. The court may revoke the order if it is satisfied that it is appropriate in all the circumstances, including any material changes and the wishes of birth parents about having PRRs given to people who have them under the order. If the court revokes the order, it must consider whether to make orders under s.11 of the 1995 Act, about PRRs.

2007 Act, s.98 referring back to s.84, and s.100

12.38

If a PO or POA is not revoked, it lasts until the child is 18, unless he or she is adopted before then.

2007 Act, s.102 and s.81

13

Adoption

This chapter deals briefly with some aspects of adoption in Scotland. Intercountry adoption and other foreign adoption matters are covered in Chapter 14.

General information

13.1

Adoption in Scotland was introduced under the Adoption (Scotland) Act 1930. There have been a number of subsequent provisions, including the Adoption (Scotland) Act 1978, which was substantially amended in 1997 by the 1995 Act. On 28 September 2009, the Adoption and Children (Scotland) Act 2007 replaced the 1978 Act. The 2007 Act followed the Adoption Policy Review Group Review, particularly the 2005 Phase II Report. The Adoption and Children Act 2002, the main legislation for England and Wales from 30 December 2005, only applies in Scotland in a few matters.

APRG 2005 Phase II Report; 2007 Act; Adoption and Children Act 2002

13.2

Adoption of a child is a legal process where a child's birth family is replaced in law by a new adoptive family, cutting off all legal ties and links with the birth family. The child becomes as if born into the adoptive family.

2007 Act, s.40

13.3

In order for a child to be adopted, every parent with PRRs must either consent to the adoption or have his or her consent dispensed with. The consent is dealt with in the adoption application or it may be done in an earlier court process for a POA. If the child is 12 or over, his or her consent is also required for adoption and for all POs and POAs.

2007 Act, s.31, s.80, s.83 and s.84, and s.32 and s.84(1)

13.4

Adoption and POA applications are dealt with in the 2007 Act. There is a range of adoption regulations, including for adoption agencies, adoption support services and allowances, accessing adoption-related information and foreign adoptions. There are National Care Standards for Adoption Agencies (see Chapter 5). There are also rules of court for the sheriff court and the Court of Session. And there are Practice Notes for each Sheriffdom, designed 'to secure the efficient management of contested applications and other proceedings under the 2007 Act' – see Further Reading.

2007 Act; Ad Ag Regs 2009; Ad Supp Regs 2009; Ad Info Regs 2009; Foreign Adoption Regs 2009; Adoption Standards; Sheriff Court Adoption Rules 2009; RCS 1994, Ch 67

13.5

All local authorities have a duty to have their own adoption agency and to provide an adoption service for their area, including provision for intercountry adoption (see Chapter 14) and adoption support (see paragraphs 13.35 to 13.38). They have to provide adoption services along with their other social work provision and with registered adoption services (see paragraph 13.7) operating in their area. From April 2004, local authority adoption agencies and registered adoption services had to be registered with and inspected by the Care Commission, and from April 2011, with its successor, the Care Inspectorate (see Chapter 5). Local authorities must also set out their adoption services in their Adoption Services Plans, which may or may not be part of their wider Children's Services Plans. The 2014 Act replaces these duties when it comes into force.

2007 Act, s.1, s.2, ss.9 to 12 and s.4; 2010 Act, s.83 and s.59; 1995 Act, s.19; 2014 Act, ss.7 to 18

Principles to be applied

13.6

The general principles (see Chapter 2) apply to all decisions made by courts and adoption agencies about adoption and POAs. These include all planning decisions by agencies. The child's welfare *throughout his or her life* is the paramount consideration. The views of the child must be sought and taken into account by agencies and courts and there must be consideration of religion, race, culture and language. Agencies and courts must also consider other options for the child, and decide on adoption only if it is the best choice. This does not mean that adoption is a last resort.

2007 Act, s.14, s.28(2) and s.84

Adoption agencies

13.7

There are two types of adoption agencies:

- **local authority adoption agencies**: see paragraph 13.5 above;
- **registered adoption services**. These are voluntary agencies providing adoption services, and must operate on a not-for-profit basis. They were formerly approved by the Scottish Executive under the 1978 Act, then registered and inspected by the Care Commission from April 2004.

Both types of agencies are now registered with and inspected by the Care Inspectorate under the 2010 Act. The Adoption Standards apply to both types of agency. All agencies must have an adoption panel unless they do not plan for children or assess adopters.

2007 Act, s.1 and s.2; 2010 Act, s.83 and s.59, including s.59(3); Adoption Standards; Ad Ag Regs 2009, regs.3 to 6

Permanence orders with authority for adoption (POAs)

13.8

A POA is an order which deals with parental consent to adoption prior to the actual adoption application. If a local authority agency is planning adoption for a child, it may choose to deal with parental consent in a POA application process, before placing with adopters, or to avoid a direct dispute between birth parents and adopters over a child already placed. However, obtaining a POA is not mandatory and it is not necessary for there to be a POA for a child before he or she is placed or adopted. For more information about POs and POAs, see Chapter 12.

2007 Act, ss.80 to 84 and s.31

Types of adoption

13.9

The 2007 Act provides for two types of adoption:

- agency adoptions; and

- relative and step-parent adoptions.

An agency adoption is where an adoption agency (see paragraph 13.7) places a child for adoption. The child will usually, but not always, be looked after – see Chapter 9. A relative adoption can be applied for by a grandparent, brother, sister, uncle, aunt of the full or half blood, and by affinity, which means by marriage or civil partnership. This includes the father of the child and his relatives if the father was not married to the mother. In a step-parent adoption, the adopter must be married to or in a civil partnership with or living in an 'enduring family relationship' with the birth parent who has PRRs. Most non-agency adoptions are step-parent ones.

2007 Act, s.75, s.119(1) and ss.29 and 30

13.10

Strictly speaking, no adoption should be arranged by anyone other than an adoption agency, unless it is a relative or step-parent one. However, in some circumstances, an adoption order may be granted when the child was not placed by an agency and is not being adopted by a close relative, even if money has been paid. For example, foster carers may seek to adopt a child who was placed with them under the fostering regulations, but not the adoption regulations. And intercountry adoptions are not agency ones, even though the adopters will have been assessed and approved by an agency – see Chapter 14. Courts are allowed to grant adoption orders even where money has been paid.

2007 Act, s.75 and s.72

13.11

In practice, most adoptions are either arranged by local authorities or other agencies, or are "relative" ones, mainly involving step-parents. The legal requirements and processes for both types of adoption are much the same, although some specific issues are different as between the two types.

Who may adopt?

13.12

There is no upper age limit for adoption, although many adoption agencies impose one, but there are lower age limits. People under 21 cannot adopt, but if the adopter is a step-parent, adoption is allowed provided the birth parent is 18, although the step-parent must be over 21. Adopters must *either* be domiciled in the UK (i.e. consider it as their long-term permanent home, even if they do not currently live there) *or* have been habitually resident in the UK for more than one year prior to the application. Where a couple are adopting, only one of them needs to be domiciled in the UK if that is the eligibility test they are using. Adopters do not have to have British nationality to be eligible to adopt.

2007 Act, ss.29 and 30

13.13

Adopters are either a couple or a single person. A couple can adopt together if they are married, or are civil partners or are living together 'in an enduring family relationship' as if married or civil partners. In step-parent adoptions, the step-parent applies on his or her own, and it is no longer possible for him or her to adopt *with* the birth parent.

2007 Act, ss.29 and 30

Who may be adopted?

13.14

For a child to be adopted, he or she must be under 18 and unmarried. However, if an adoption petition has been lodged before a child's 18th birthday, it may be dealt with and granted even after the child reaches that age. The child may be of any nationality. As indicated in paragraph 13.3, the consent of a child aged 12 or over is formally required before the order may be granted. This may only be dispensed with if the court considers the child is incapable of consenting.

2007 Act, s.28(4) and s.32

13.15

A child must have lived with the applicants or one of them before an adoption order may be granted. If the child is being adopted by a step-parent or a relative, or the adoption is an agency one, the child must be at least 19 weeks old before the adoption can be granted, *and* have lived with the applicants for the previous 13 weeks. This means that an adoption application may be lodged in court for a child under 19 weeks, and who has lived with the applicant for less than 13 weeks, but the order cannot be granted before then.

2007 Act, s.15(1), (2) and (3)

13.16

Where an application to adopt a child is not made by a relative (as defined in the 2007 Act – see paragraph 13.9) or step-parent and the child has not been placed for adoption by an agency, the child must be at least one year old before the order is made and have lived for at least one year with the applicants. This would include foster carer applications and most but not all adoptions from abroad. The rules about this matter in intercountry adoption are covered in Chapter 14.

2007 Act, s.15(1) and (4)

Pre-court procedures: non-agency adoptions

13.17

In *all* non-agency adoptions, including relative and step-parent ones, and intercountry adoptions (see Chapter 14), applicants must notify the local authority where they live about their intention to adopt. The notification must be made at least three months before the adoption order is granted. The local authority must prepare and lodge in court a report about the family, the child and all the circumstances of the case. This is often referred to as a "s.19 Report". There are detailed court rules about what the report should cover.

2007 Act, ss.18 and 19; Sheriff Court Adoption Rules 2009, r.8(4) to (7); RCS r.67.8(4) to (7)

13.18

In some step-parent or relative adoptions, the child has come from overseas and there may be some international aspects to the adoption, such as the need to obtain written consent from a birth parent who resides abroad. These adoptions are not intercountry ones and the adopters do not have to have been assessed under the intercountry adoption rules – see Chapter 14. Similarly, when a child is brought into the UK from overseas by people who have been living and working abroad, and who then wish to adopt the child, that is not an intercountry adoption. Court rules have provisions about having agreements signed abroad when this is necessary.

Sheriff Court Adoption Rules 2009, r.13(3)(c); RCS r.67.13(3)(c)

Pre-court procedures: agency adoptions

13.19

Where a local authority agency wishes to place a child for adoption, with or without a POA application, there are complicated regulations about procedures and timescales. The adoption agency's crucial stages are the agency adoption panel and the agency decision-maker. No child may be placed by an agency unless its adoption panel has considered the plans for that child and made a recommendation that adoption, with or without a POA, is the best plan for the child. In every case, disputed or undisputed, the agency then has timescales within which it must make a formal decision and notify this to birth parents and others. If the birth parents indicate within a certain time that they are in agreement with the plan for adoption and/or a POA, the agency may go ahead without further timescales. If, however, the parents refuse to agree, or do not return the notifications within a set time, the agency is tied by strict timescales. It must apply for a POA or ensure that an adoption application is lodged by adoptive parents within very short timescales. There are also general duties on agencies about placing a child, about information gathering, notifications and visiting.

Ad Ag Regs 2009, reg. 6, regs.12 to 17 and regs.20 to 23; also reg.18 and regs.23A to 25A

13.20

When a child is subject to a CSO and adoption plans, with or without a POA, there are additional requirements. The child must be referred to a children's hearing for a review of the CSO and consideration of the plans. The hearing provides a written report on the plans, usually called "advice". Where the parent does not agree, and/or the hearing members disagree with the plans, there are detailed timescales which apply.

2011 Act, s.131, s.137, s.138 and s.141; and Ad Ag Regs 2009, regs.22 and 23

13.21

In all agency adoptions, the placing agency (and this includes English, Welsh and Northern Irish agencies when a child is placed from outwith Scotland) must prepare and lodge a report for the court. This is often referred to as a "s.17 Report", but it is almost the same as a "s.19 Report" – see paragraph 13.17. There are the same detailed court rules about what the report should cover.

2007 Act, s.17; Sheriff Court Adoption Rules 2009, r.8(4) to (7); RCS r.67.8(4) to (7)

Court procedures

13.22

Adoption may be applied for in the sheriff court or the Court of Session. In every application, whether agreed or not, the court has to be satisfied about a number of conditions and considerations, including the principles set out in Chapter 2 – see paragraph 13.31. Court procedures for adoption, and all POAs and POs, are very similar – see Chapter 12, paragraphs 12.15 to 12.28. Where the child resides in Scotland at the time an adoption application is made, it may be heard in the Court of Session or in the local sheriff court. The decision about where to apply is made by the adopter making the application. Most cases are dealt with in the sheriff court. If the child resides outwith Scotland at the time the application is made, it can only be heard in the Court of Session.

2007 Act, s.118

13.23

Forms are provided with the court rules for adoption, PO and POA applications or petitions. These are in appendices to the rules, but the easiest way to obtain up-to-date versions is from the courts directly, or from the Scottish Courts website – see Further Reading. Forms are completed and lodged in court, along with other documents such as the child's birth certificate. The s.17 or s.19 report (see paragraphs 13.17 and 13.21) should also be lodged at the same time. In PO and POA cases, the local authority also have to lodge a detailed report with every court application – see Chapter 12, paragraph 12.14.

Sheriff Court Adoption Rules 2009, r.8, especially r.8(3)(d) and (e); RCS r.67.8, especially r.67.8(3)(d) and (e)

13.24

Once the adoption petition is lodged, court rules have timetables for dealing with the different stages of the application, particularly in disputed cases. The court arranges a preliminary hearing to take place within eight weeks. The applicant must then intimate the application and the hearing date to the birth parents and anyone else the court thinks should receive notice. Anyone who wishes to oppose the application must lodge a form of response saying this, within 21 days. The court also appoints a curator, and in most cases, a reporting officer.

Sheriff Court Adoption Rules 2009, rr.11, rr.14 to 16A, r.18, r.18A, r.19, r.20 and r.22; RCS r.67.11, rr.67.14 and 67.15 and rr.67.17 and 67.18

13.25

The reporting officer is mainly concerned with the consent or non-consent to the adoption by the parents and by any child aged 12 or over. When parents and/or the child agree to the adoption, the reporting officer obtains their formal written consents. When there is no agreement, he or she reports this to the court. The reporting officer should report back to the court within four weeks. No reporting officer is appointed if there is a POA and the child is under 12.

Sheriff Court Adoption Rules 2009, rr.11 and 12; RCS rr.67.11 and 67.12

13.26

The court also appoints a curator who should report back to the court within four weeks. The curator is often the same person as the reporting officer, but not always. The curator is an independent person providing a view of the case from the perspective of the child's welfare. He or she must also give the child's views to the court, provided the child wishes to give them to the curator.

Sheriff Court Adoption Rules 2009, rr.11 and 12; RCS rr.67.11 and 67.12

13.27

At the preliminary hearing, if there is no opposition to the application, the court may grant the order or continue the matter for further information, etc. Even when the birth parents have consented, the court must be satisfied about the principles in the 2007 Act – see Chapter 2. If there is no opposition but the birth parents have not formally consented, the court will have to be satisfied that the consent may be dispensed with, although there may not be a full evidential proof – see paragraphs 13.29 and 13.30.

2007 Act, s.14, s.28(2) and s.31; Sheriff Court Adoption Rules 2009, r.18; RCS, r.67.17

13.28

If the birth parents are opposing the application, the adopters must lodge a brief statement of the facts they will be relying on, and this must then be answered by or on behalf of the birth parents. A proof hearing will be fixed, which should be within 16 weeks. A pre-proof hearing is also arranged in most cases, to enable the court to find out if the parties are properly prepared. In the sheriff court, Practice Notes for each Sheriffdom give further directions about procedures to be followed – see Further Reading.

Sheriff Court Adoption Rules 2009, r.16A and rr.18 to 20; RCS, rr.67.17 and 67.18

13.29

Before any child may be adopted, every parent with PRRs must:

- formally consent to the adoption; *or*
- have his or her consent dispensed with in the adoption application on the basis of one or more of the five grounds in s.31(3) to (6); *or*

- have had his or her consent fully dealt with in an earlier court case, such as a POA, or a freeing order (in Northern Ireland); *or*

- have had his or her consent partially dealt with in earlier proceedings under the Adoption and Children Act 2002 (in England or Wales), and he or she does not dispute the adoption application.

2007 Act, s.31

13.30

There are five grounds for dispensing with consent, and they are the same as those used in POA applications – see Chapter 12, paragraph 12.24. They are different from those in the previous legislation and are also different from those used in England and Wales under the 2002 Act. The grounds are:

1. the parent or guardian is dead, s.31(3)(a);

2. the parent or guardian cannot be found or is incapable of consenting, s.31(3)(b);

3. the parent or guardian

   - has parental responsibilities or rights *or*

   - cannot, in the court's opinion, 'satisfactorily...discharge' those parental responsibilities or exercise those parental rights *and*

   - 'is likely to continue to be unable to do so', s.31(4);

4. the parent or guardian

   - has lost all parental responsibilities or rights through a permanence order which does not give authority for adoption (i.e. a PO not a POA) *and*

   - is 'unlikely' to be given back such responsibilities or rights, s.31(5);

5. where neither of the previous two grounds (i.e. 3 and 4) apply, the child's welfare 'otherwise requires the consent to be dispensed with', s.31(3)(d).

2007 Act, s.31(3) to (6)

13.31
___

If the birth parents are disputing the adoption, the adopters have to ask the court to dispense with their consent on one of the grounds listed in s.31 of the 2007 Act, if consent has not already been dealt with in an earlier court case. The court considers evidence in order to decide whether to dispense with consent on one of the grounds listed in paragraph 13.30. If the court is satisfied evidentially, it still has to decide on the basis of the welfare and other principles whether to dispense with the consent, and then whether to grant the adoption. The court's decision about the application (apart from whether there is sufficient evidence to dispense with consent) is governed by the principles in the 2007 Act – see Chapter 2.

13.32
___

Where a court grants an adoption order and the child is subject to a compulsory supervision order, the court must revoke the CSO unless it thinks that the child still needs compulsory measures under the Children's Hearing system.

2007 Act, s.36

13.33
___

When a court grants or refuses to grant an adoption order, there is a right of appeal. If the application was made in the sheriff court, an appeal may be made to the Sheriff Principal and/or to the Inner House of the Court of Session. If the application was made in the Court of Session, an appeal may be made to the Inner House of the Court of Session. A further appeal is possible to the Supreme Court.

Effects of an adoption order

13.34
___

When an adoption order is granted in favour of a couple or an individual, that person or those persons hold all the PRRs over the child as if the child had been born to them. The birth parents, if they have not previously lost all PRRs through a POA process, now lose all formal responsibilities for and rights to their child. There may be ongoing contact arrangements, particularly for indirect ones like "letterbox contact", but these are usually just by agreement with the adopters. It is possible to have a contact condition attached to an adoption order, but this is not very common and will normally only happen in 'exceptional' circumstances. After an adoption, birth parents cannot use s.11 of the 1995 Act except to apply for a contact order, and they must have the leave of the court before they may even go ahead and apply fully.

2007 Act, s.40 and s.28(3); 1995 Act, s.11(3) to (6) as amended by the 2007 Act

Adoption support

13.35

Local authority adoption agencies have a duty to provide adoption support to a wide range of people affected by adoption, including adopted children and adults, adopters and their children, and the birth families of adopted children and adults. The adoption support system was widened under the 2007 Act with the intention of extending the system and ensuring greater uniformity of services. The Ad Supp Regulations 2009 and the 2007 Act Guidance are also relevant. The system is complex and covers agency and non-agency adoptions.

2007 Act, s.1, ss.9 to 12 and ss.45 to 52; Ad Supp Regs 2009; 2007 Act Guidance

13.36

The 2007 Act provides for assessment of needs for support services, and for the provision of these services. Children being adopted, their adopters and their birth parents may receive support services without assessments of their need for these. There are adoption support plans, which are possible for any family with adopted children under 18, whether the adoption is an agency or non-agency one. Adoption allowances are available for agency adopters in certain circumstances.

2007 Act, s.1, ss.9 to 12 and ss.45 to 52; Ad Supp Regs 2009

13.37

A wide range of other people are also eligible for assessments of their needs for adoption support, and service provision if there is need. Overall, these duties are wide and apply to the whole of the local authorities where people seeking services live. In addition, they apply to all adoptions, agency and non-agency, past and present. For example, when a birth parent wants help about tracing a child who has been adopted, he or she is entitled to an assessment of need for support by the local authority in whose area he or she currently lives.

2007 Act, s.1, ss.9 to 12; Ad Supp Regs 2009, particularly regs.5 to 9

13.38

A local authority agency will often place a child for adoption outside its geographical area. The placing agency's adoption support duties continue for three years from the date of the adoption, to the child, adopters and the birth parents. After that, the duties transfer to the local authority agency where the family live, although the placing agency has discretion to continue providing support. However, if an adoption allowance is being paid, that remains the responsibility of the placing agency.

Ad Supp Regs 2009, particularly reg.4

Access to birth records

13.39

Adoption agency records are exempt from the subject access provisions of the DPA 1998, so there is no right of subject access to them. The exemptions are in the Data Protection (Miscellaneous Subject Access Exemptions) Order 2000, S.I. 2000/419, as amended by the Data Protection (Miscellaneous Subject Access Exemptions) (Amendment) Order 2000, SI 2000/1865, and further amended and updated for the 2007 Act by Schedule 1, paragraph 22 of the Adoption and Children (Scotland) Act 2007 (Consequential Modifications) Order 2011, SI 2011/1740. Instead, adoption agency records are accessed under the Ad Info Regs 2009.

13.40

In Scotland, when an adopted person reaches 16, he or she has automatic rights of access to:

- his or her original birth certificate;

- his or her court process from the adoption, and from any POA as well; and

- his or her adoption agency records, if the adoption was an agency one.

Counselling services are available but optional. An adopted person will be entitled to adoption support services to help him or her find this information and decide what other steps, if any, to take. He or she should formally request support services to help access any adoption agency records, but the other information may be sought without this, although support may be helpful.

2007 Act, s.55; Sheriff Court Adoption Rules 2009, r.25(2)(a) and r.39(2) and (3)(a); RCS, r.67.21(2)(a) and r.67.33(2) and (3)(a); Ad Info Regs 2009, reg.3(1) and reg.4

13.41

If there are adoption agency records for an adopted person under 16, the agency has discretion to disclose information to him or her. Adoption agencies also have a general discretion to provide access to their records as part of their functions as agencies, including to other local authorities which have been approached by adopted people for help in accessing their records.

Ad Info Regs 2009, reg.3(2) to (5), and regs.4 to 6

13.42

There is no right of access to information for birth parents, but there is an entitlement to an assessment for adoption support services, including counselling, from their local authority agency. Other members of birth families and people affected by adoption are also entitled to assessments for adoption support services. These duties clearly cover providing help to birth families about ways of tracing family members who have been adopted.

2007 Act, s.1, s.9 and s.10

14

Foreign adoptions

This chapter gives some basic information about foreign adoptions, including intercountry adoptions. It deals with two situations:

1. where a child from overseas is adopted into Scotland, usually referred to as intercountry adoption; and

2. where a Scottish child leaves the UK for adoption in an overseas country.

14.1

Some adoptions have international aspects, e.g. step-parent adoption of a child from overseas now living in the UK with his or her parent and step-parent; step-parent adoption by someone domiciled in the UK but living abroad; and adoption by people who have returned to live in the UK after working abroad, where they adopted a child but that adoption is not recognised here. Although there may be difficulties in such cases, like obtaining parental consent from abroad or other logistical problems, these are not overseas or intercountry adoptions, but are ordinary "domestic" adoptions.

Intercountry adoption

14.2

Intercountry adoption is where a child from overseas is adopted into Scotland. Although the practice and policy about intercountry adoption are the same throughout the UK, there are a number of detailed differences between the system in Scotland and that for England and Wales. As a result, not all legal details provided on a UK basis are correct for Scotland.

14.3

Intercountry adoption is the term used by professionals, adoption agencies, central government and those who adopt children from outwith the UK. It refers to adoption where:

- the adopter(s) reside in the UK; *and*
- the child resides in a country outside the UK (the State of origin); *and*
- the adopter(s) either:
    - bring the child into the UK for the purposes of adoption *or*
    - adopt the child in his or her State of origin, *and* that order is recognised as adoption in UK law.

14.4

Other adoptions have international aspects, e.g. adoption of a step-child from overseas now living in the UK; or by adopters who have returned to live in the UK after working abroad, where they adopted a child but that adoption is not recognised here. However, these are not intercountry adoptions – see paragraph 14.1.

Background

14.5

Intercountry adoption in the UK was the subject of good practice procedures for some years but the system had no statutory basis. During the 1990s, there were increasing concerns about abuses and the UK had to legislate to enable it to ratify the Hague Convention.

14.6

The 1999 Act was passed to provide a regulatory system for intercountry adoption from the three groups of countries listed below. There are differences in the rules for each of the three groups of cases, although the underlying assessment processes are the same. In Scotland, the 1999 Act amended and added to the 1978 Act for intercountry purposes and provided for regulations and court rules to be made for these adoptions. The regulations, court rules and Commencement Orders for Scotland were different from those for England and Wales. Most but not all of the 1999 Act has been replaced in Scotland by the provisions of the 2007 Act.

1999 Act, as amended by and partially repealed by the 2007 Act

Types of countries from which children are adopted

14.7

There are three different types of countries from which intercountry adoptions are arranged, that is, three types of States of origin for children. The type of country of origin affects whether there has to be an adoption application in the UK after the child comes here. The three types of countries of origin are:

- **Convention countries:** countries that have implemented the Hague Convention. In some cases, the child will be adopted in the State of origin, in others adoption will be in the UK;

- **designated list countries:** countries on the designated list, whose adoption orders are recognised in the UK. There is no need for an adoption application here;

- **non-Convention/non-designated countries:** countries that are neither Hague Convention nor designated list ones. When the child enters the UK, it is necessary to apply to adopt here.

14.8

The Scottish Government and Department for Education (DfE) Intercountry adoption websites (see Further Reading) list Convention and designated countries under "Frequently asked questions". The list of designated countries has been restated with effect from 3 January 2014. The Adoption (Designation of Overseas Adoptions) Order 1973 as varied by the Adoption (Designation of Overseas Adoptions) (Variation) (Scotland) Order 1995 has been revoked although that does not affect any adoption designated under it as an overseas one prior to 3 January 2014. There is an equivalent order for England and Wales.

Adoption (Recognition of Overseas Adoptions) (Scotland) Regulations 2013, SSI 2013/310, as amended by the Adoption (Recognition of Overseas Adoptions) (Scotland) Amendment Regulations 2013, SSI 2013/335

Special restrictions on countries

14.9

The Scottish Government have the power to make regulations imposing restrictions on adoptions from overseas countries as they see necessary. These restrictions are to make sure that, when there are concerns about adoption practices in other countries, arrangements to adopt from these may be prohibited or restricted. There are special restrictions in relation to adoptions from Haiti, Nepal, Cambodia and Guatemala.

2007 Act, ss.62 to 65; Adoptions with a Foreign Element (Special Restrictions on Adoptions from Abroad) (Scotland) Regulations 2008, SSI 2008/303

Intercountry adoption processes: pre-court

14.10

In adoption from all three types of countries, prospective adopters, including close relatives, must have a home study prepared and be assessed as intercountry adopters by an adoption agency, either a local authority or a voluntary agency. Local authorities must provide an intercountry service. The assessment cannot be done by an independent social worker who is not commissioned by an adoption agency. The home study is for adoption from a specific country. After assessment, the agency takes the prospective adopters to its adoption panel and then the agency decision-maker approves them as intercountry adopters for the specific country, or does not approve them. When there is approval, the papers are sent by the agency to the Scottish Government.

2007 Act, s.1; Foreign Adoption Regs 2009; Ad Ag Regs 2009

14.11

If the proposed adoption is from a Convention country, the Scottish Government is the Central Authority. It processes the papers and if it agrees that an application can go ahead, the papers are passed to the Home Office for immigration clearance. Once this is completed, the Scottish Government as Central Authority passes the papers to the Central Authority for the State of origin and the prospective adopters can make arrangements there.

14.12

If the proposed adoption is from a designated or non-Convention/non-designated country, the process is the same, except the Central Authority is the Department for Education (DfE) in London. So the papers go from the Scottish Government to the DfE and then on to the Home Office.

14.13

After completion of the arrangements in the State of origin, the adopters bring the child into the UK. If the adopters have not gone through the above processes, they may be guilty of an offence under the 2007 Act or the Foreign Adoption Regs 2009. There are four possible situations on return to the UK. The child will have been:

1. adopted in a Convention country (a Convention adoption);

2. brought in from a Convention country for adoption here by way of a Convention adoption order application;

3. adopted in a designated list country;

4. brought in from a non-Convention/non-designated country for adoption here under the 2007 Act, s.29 or 30.

2007 Act, s.58 and 61; Foreign Adoption Regs 2009, reg.53; 2007 Act, s.119(1); 1999 Act

Intercountry adoption processes: court

14.14

In the first or third situations, there is no court application here, as both types of adoption are recognized in UK law. In the second or fourth situations, there has to be an adoption application here. It is also necessary in these two situations for the adopters to contact their local authority to advise that the child is living with them and give notice of:

- a private fostering arrangement under the 1984 Act; *and*

- their intention to adopt, under s.18 of the 2007 Act.

1984 Act; 2007 Act, s.18

14.15

If the child has been brought in for adoption from a Convention country, a Convention adoption order application is made under the Foreign Adoption Regs 2009. This can be in the sheriff court or the Court of Session, and there are specific court rules for these applications.

Foreign Adoption Regs 2009, reg.53; Sheriff Court Adoption Rules 2009, rr.28 to 30; RCS, rr.67.24 to 67.27

14.16

If the child has been brought in for adoption from a non-Convention/non-designated country, the case is similar to a domestic application, under the 1978 Act and the normal court rules.

2007 Act, s.29 or 30; Sheriff Court Adoption Rules 2009, rr.8 to 27; RCS rr.67.8 to 67.23

Residence period required before adoption can be granted in Scotland

14.17

There are rules about how long a child must live with both adopters before an order can be granted (not applied for). These are in s.15 of the 2007 Act. The period for intercountry adoptions is six months residence.

2007 Act, s.15, particularly s.15(5)

Entry clearance and acquiring British citizenship

14.18

The Immigration Rules are extremely complex and specialist immigration advice should be sought. The UK Border Agency has a leaflet about intercountry adoption on its website, dated 2008. All intercountry adopters, including from Convention countries, should ensure that they have entry clearance for the child, in advance of bringing him or her into the UK.

14.19

In stranger intercountry adoptions, the basic rules about citizenship are relatively straightforward, and depend on the type of State of origin and where the adoption took place, i.e. in the UK or abroad.

- Convention adoption abroad confers British citizenship other than by descent (BC-OTB), provided one adopter is a British citizen and both are 'habitually resident' in the UK.

- Convention adoption *and* non-Convention/non-designated adoption in the UK confers BC-OTB, provided one adopter is a British citizen.

- Designated adoption abroad does not automatically confer BC-OTBD. However, the adopters may apply to register the child as a British citizen under the British Nationality Act 1981, and if successful, BC-OTBD will be conferred.

Registration of foreign adoptions

14.20

The Registration of Foreign Adoptions (Scotland) Regulations 2003 came into force on 1 June 2003. They allow adopters who have adopted abroad from Convention and designated countries to apply for an entry in the Scottish Adopted Children Register. The Registrar General will issue an extract from the Register. When a child has been adopted abroad, and the adoption is recognised in the UK, an entry in the Register may be made and an "ordinary" Scottish Extract Birth Certificate will be issued. The 2003 Regulations may be used for foreign adoptions which took place before June 2003.

Registration of Foreign Adoptions (Scotland) Regulations 2003, SSI 2003/67

Arrangements for Scottish children to be adopted overseas

14.21

These are covered by ss.59 and 60 of the 2007 Act, and the Foreign Adoptions Regs 2009 are also relevant. The provisions are complex and their effect is different from that under the 1978 Act, which allowed close relatives to take a child out of the UK for adoption abroad.

2007 Act, ss.59 and 60; Foreign Adoptions Regs 2009

14.22

It is an offence to take a 'protected child' out of Great Britain for adoption overseas or to make arrangements for such an adoption. However, such an adoption is permitted if the child is taken out of Great Britain under a s.59 order or the equivalent provisions in other UK legislation. A 'protected child' is a child who is habitually resident in the UK or is a Commonwealth citizen.

2007 Act, s.60

14.23

An s.59 order allows a child to be adopted abroad after a court application in Scotland. It gives the prospective adopters parental responsibilities and rights. An application may be made in the sheriff court or the Court of Session and the court rules treat them almost the same as domestic adoptions. However, a s.59 order cannot be made unless requirements in that section and the Foreign Adoptions Regs 2009 have been met. These include that the child has to have lived with the applicants for at least 10 weeks before the order may be applied for. If a local authority adoption agency are planning adoption for a child outside the UK, they will have to seek a POA before the prospective adopters apply for the s.59 order.

2007 Act, s.59; Foreign Adoption Regs 2009

Further reading

Books and publications

Adoption Policy Review Group (2005) *Adoption: Better choices for our children – Report of Phase II*, Edinburgh: Scottish Executive. Available on the Scottish Government website, under Publications, 29 June 2005.

Butterworths (1997 onwards) *Scottish Family Law Service*, London: Butterworths/LexisNexis. This is a loose-leaf publication, updated every six months.

Disclosure Scotland (2012) *Updated Guidance on Foster Care, Kinship Care and Adoption*. Available from www.disclosurescotland.co.uk – click on Publications.

Green (1997 onwards) *Scottish Family Law Legislation* and *Scottish Social Work Legislation*, Edinburgh: W Green/Thomson. These are annotated statutes, etc, published in loose-leaf form and updated regularly.

McNeill PGB and Morag J (2010) *Adoption of Children in Scotland* (4th edition), Edinburgh: W Green/Sweet & Maxwell

Norrie K McK (2004) *Children (Scotland) Act 1995 – Annotated version* (2nd edition), Edinburgh: W Green/Sweet & Maxwell

Norrie K McK (2013) *Children's Hearings in Scotland* (3rd edition), Edinburgh: W Green/Sweet & Maxwell

Plumtree A (2003) *Choices for Children*, Edinburgh: Scottish Executive for the Adoption Policy Review Group. Available on the Scottish Government website under Publications, 11 September 2003.

Plumtree A (2011) *Permanence and Adoption for Children: A guide to the Adoption and Children (Scotland) Act 2007*, London: BAAF

The Scottish Executive (2004) *Supporting Young People Leaving Care in Scotland: Regulations and guidance on services for young people ceasing to be looked after by local authorities,* Edinburgh: TSO. Available on the Scottish Government website under Publications, 31 March 2004.

The Scottish Executive (2005) *Secure and Safe Homes for our Most Vulnerable Children: Scottish Executive proposals for action on the APRG Phase II Report*, Edinburgh: Scottish Executive. Available on the Scottish Government website under Publications, 30 June 2005.

The Scottish Government (2010) *National Guidance for Child Protection in Scotland 2010,* Edinburgh: Scottish Government. Available on the Scottish Government website under Publications, 13 December 2010. It has been amended and added to and will be issued in a refreshed version in early 2014.

The Scottish Government (2011) *Guidance on the Looked After Children (Scotland) Regulations 2009 and the Adoption and Children (Scotland) Act 2007*, Edinburgh: Scottish Government. Available on the Scottish Government website under Publications, 10 March 2011.

The Scottish Government (2013) *Private Fostering in Scotland: Practice guidance for local authority children's services*, Edinburgh: Scottish Government. Available on the Scottish Government website under Publications, 29 November 2013.

The Scottish Office (1997) *Scotland's Children: The Children (Scotland) Act 1995, Regulations and Guidance: Volume 1: Support and protection for children and their families*, Edinburgh: HMSO. Available on the Scottish Government website under Publications, 12 October 2004.

Thomson JM (2011) *Family Law in Scotland* (6th edition), Edinburgh: Bloomsbury Professional

Wilkinson A and Norrie K McN (2013) *Parent and Child* (3rd edition Norrie K McN), Edinburgh: W Green

Useful websites

British Association for Adoption and Fostering, BAAF
www.baaf.org.uk

Care Inspectorate
www.scswis.com/
Responsible for the regulation, registration and inspection of Scottish care services. There is a link on the Home page to the National Care Standards.

CELCIS, Centre of Excellence for Looked After Children in Scotland
www.celcis.org/

Children's Hearings Scotland, CHS
www.chscotland.gov.uk/
Responsible for panel members for the Children's Hearing system, including recruitment, training, support and monitoring.

COPFS, Crown Office and Procurator Fiscal Service
www.crownoffice.gov.uk/
Responsible for criminal prosecutions in Scotland.

DfE intercountry adoption website
www.education.gov.uk/childrenandyoungpeople/families/adoption/ intercountryadoption
The Department for Education is responsible for adoption in England. The information about countries and adopting from them is helpful, but the legal input should be treated with caution, as many provisions are different in Scotland.

Disclosure Scotland
www.disclosurescotland.co.uk/

Information Commissioner for the UK
www.informationcommissioner.gov.uk/
Responsible for monitoring the DPA 1998 and also for FOI for UK-wide public authorities.

Intercountry Adoption Centre
www.icacentre.org.uk/

Safeguarders Panel

www.children1st.org.uk/what-we-do/our-services/search-our-services/
safeguarders-panel/

Children 1st manages the Safeguarders Panel, part of the Children's Hearing system. There is no specific website, but there is information on the Children 1st website under 'Our Services'.

Scottish Children's Reporter Administration, SCRA

www.scra.gov.uk/home/index.cfm

SCRA is responsible for the reporters' service in the Children's Hearing system.

Scottish Courts Service

www.scotcourts.gov.uk/

Scottish Government

www.scotland.gov.uk/Home

Scottish Government Intercountry Adoption

www.scotland.gov.uk/Topics/People/Young-People/protecting/lac/adoption/
incountryadoption

Scottish Information Commissioner

www.itspublicknowledge.info/home/

The Commissioner is responsible for FOI for Scottish public authorities.

Scottish Throughcare and Aftercare Forum

www.scottishthroughcare.org.uk

UK Border Agency

www.ukba.homeoffice.gov.uk/

For information about intercountry adoption, use the search function. NB: the website stated in 2013 that its content will be moved in due course to the Government's digital service at www.gov.uk.

WithScotland

http://withscotland.org/

The main Scottish website for child protection information and developments.

Specific online resources

Court Rules online

All the Scottish court rules are available on the Scottish Courts website at www.scotcourts.gov.uk/home under Rules and Practice, Rules of Court. Click on Court of Session Rules or Sheriff Court – Civil Procedure Rules. The page for sheriff court rules includes the Ordinary Cause Rules (OCR) and the Sheriff Court Adoption Rules 2009.

Sheriff Court Practice Notes online

Sheriff Court Practice Notes are issued from time to time by individual Sheriffs Principal for his or her Sheriffdom. They are available on the Scottish Courts website at www.scotcourts.gov.uk/home under Rules and Practice, and click on Sheriff Court Practice Notes (Civil). They are listed by year and by Sheriffdom. Those for proceedings under the Adoption and Children (Scotland) Act 2007 were all published in 2009.

Judgments online

Judgments in Court of Session cases and some sheriff court cases, from September 1998 onwards, are available on the Scottish Courts website at www.scotcourts.gov.uk/home under Search Judgements

Legislation online

All Acts, regulations, orders and court rules are available on the Legislation website at www.legislation.gov.uk/
Click on Browse at www.legislation.gov.uk/browse and the page shows all types of legislation, which you can access by clicking on the relevant link. These include:

- UK Public Acts, made at Westminster

- Acts of the Scottish Parliament

- Scottish Statutory Instruments, SSIs, including court rules

- Statutory Instruments, SIs.